A Woman's POWER

THREADS that BIND us to GOD

A Woman's POWER

THREADS that BIND us to GOD

FAY A. KLINGLER

CFI
AN IMPRINT OF CEDAR FORT, INC.
SPRINGVILLE, UT

ISBN 13: 978-1-4621-1029-2

Published by CFI, an imprint of Cedar Fort, Inc., 2373 W. 700 S., Springville, UT 84663
Distributed by Cedar Fort, Inc., www.cedarfort.com

LIBRARY OF CONGRESS CATALOGING-IN-PUBLICATION DATA

Klingler, Fay A., author.
A woman's power : threads that bind us to God / Fay A. Klingler.
pages cm
ISBN 978-1-4621-1029-2
1. Women--Religious aspects--Church of Jesus Christ of Latter-day Saints. 2. Mormon women--Religious life. I. Title.

BX8643.W66K55 2012
248.8'43--dc23

2011049312

Cover design by Angela D. Olsen
Cover design © 2012 by Lyle Mortimer
Edited and typeset by Michelle Stoll

Printed in the United States of America

10 9 8 7 6 5 4 3 2 1

Printed on acid-free paper

Praise for

A WOMAN'S POWER: THREADS THAT BIND US TO GOD

"Fay Klingler is not only well-grounded in the gospel, but her stories, quotes, and wisdom offer hope and help to make our lives more deeply meaningful."

—Linda Eyre, Author of the #1 New York Times
bestseller *Teaching Your Children Values*

"For someone seeking tried and true solutions to real-life problems, your answers could very well lie within the pages of *A Woman's Power: Threads that Bind Us to God*. Fay has accurately captured the essence of our potential as women and has carefully and expertly guided us to discover that power within ourselves."

—Marcia Z. Ford, Former National President
of American Mothers, Inc.

"Inspiring and uplifting, this book offers warm encouragement, positive spiritual solutions, and fresh, enlightening insights into eternal truths."

—Carolyn Campbell, Award-winning author,
Reunited: True Stories of Long-Lost Siblings Who Find Each Other Again

"The principles taught in this book are true and powerful. When they are exercised in each individual's life, she will feel a greater peace and a greater capacity to confront life's challenges and strengthen her relationship with God. Fay Klingler illustrates these principles through interesting stories and scripture that will capture your attention and bring them to life. I highly recommend this motivational read."

—Kimberly Toronto,
Licensed Clinical Social Worker

"Anyone seeking insight, hope, and a deeper understanding of who she is and the power that is within her will value this book. Thank you, Fay Klingler, for being an instrument in the Lord's hands."

—Diane M. Stuart, former Director of the Office on Violence Against Women in the US Department of Justice

"This book encourages all women to thoughtfully ponder the opportunity to build a powerful and more trusting relationship with our Father in Heaven, and to follow specific steps to confirm our identity as Daughters of God, with inherent rights to personal safety and the ability to embrace life with confidence and joy."

—Merilyn H. Wright, MS,
Licensed Professional Counselor

"As a 37-year practicing marriage and family therapist, I fully anticipated from the preliminary title of this book—*Threads of Power and Safety*—to read instruction for women on being empowered and safe from the control of men. But it has nothing to do with the negatives of life. It is all about being in the cradle of the Lord's arms through righteous living, but living in a practical, simplistic, and attainable way. . . . Fay does a marvelous job in giving women patterns for life, a tapestry of threads for safety and power."

—Dr. J. Kent Griffiths, Doctor of Social Work, Licensed Clinical
Social Worker, & Licensed Marriage and Family Therapist

Fay Klingler . . . gives both women and men great spiritual insights as to how we can cope with our mortal challenges. Her use of inspirational stories and quotes helps give guidance and practical application of the principles she teaches. "With God's assistance we cannot fail." She tells us how and why.

—Cynthia Terry,
Church Building Hosting Director

True principles, illustrated with real life examples, that is the way to truly teach. Fay Klingler's book, *A Woman's Power: Threads that Bind Us to God*, is filled with inspiring quotes, stories, and examples that will inspire women to more closely include the Lord as part of their lives. As I read, I was making connections to my own life story and relationship with my Heavenly Father and motivated to strengthen my ties with Him.

—Macy Robison, Creator & Performer,
Children Will Listen: Reflections on Motherhood

As I read *A Woman's Power: Threads that Bind Us to God*, I was pleased to find the answers to life's problems come from our understanding of who we are and how we respond to that knowledge. Fay Klingler's testimony throughout the book speaks of the power we have to take charge of our lives and the power we have to respond to what we have no control over. This book definitely has my endorsement!

—Toni Fabrizio, Former Church Building Hosting Director

As the bishop of a Young Single Adult ward, I see, interview, and associate with beautiful young women on a regular basis. In this chaotic world these women are challenged on every side. . . . Fay Klingler's book, *A Woman's Power: Threads that Bind Us to God*, is just the kind of book these young women need for strength to get through the day, the week, their lives. I'd like a stack of her books to hand out to each of my lovely sisters—the ones who are succeeding as well as the ones who struggle.

Thank you, Sister Klingler. Your wise words will help a great many women.

—Bishop Curtis F. Dickerson

Acknowledgments

I express appreciation to everyone who contributed to the writing of this book. I am particularly grateful for my best friend and companion—my husband Larry N. Klingler—whose patient support warms my heart every single day.

I'm continually indebted to my wonderful parents, Miles and June Alldredge. They have anchored and sustained me through their steadfast examples, truly living the gospel. I love my family—children, grandchildren, and extended family—and thank them for their contributions and encouragement. And I offer an immense thank you to my dear friend Lori Frischknecht for consistently helping me with ideas and edits throughout the writing process.

Contents

CHAPTER 1

Introduction

For as he thinketh in his heart, so is he . . .
Apply thine heart unto instruction, and thine ears to the words of knowledge.
—*Proverbs 23:7, 12*

Woven in the tapestry of life are certain powerful threads. As long as they adhere to life's experiences and are consistently followed, come what may, they form a simple, proven pattern that guarantees success and safety. What success? Fulfilling our purposes or missions on this earth and securing happiness in the eternities. What safety? The sustaining power of being guided by the Spirit, carried by the Lord.

Now, I said "simple" when I described that proven pattern, and it is. But that doesn't mean it's easy. Every woman knows too well the many worldly distractions, the barrage of temptations . . . and far too many know extreme heartache and live in dangerous environments. We're all true pioneers of a sort.

One day I drove to my son Marcus's home to deliver a family history I had just completed for him. I mentioned something about how difficult it was for our pioneer ancestors and how amazing it was for them to remain faithful under such hardships. His response stunned me. With passion he said, "Which is more damaging to your salvation—immorality or suffering death due to hunger? In some parts of the world, they're both ever-present issues. Hardship due to exposure affects your attitude and faith, but getting caught up in the base deconstruction of society and immorality while sitting in a warm, cozy house is far more powerful and seductive."

News headlines every day showcase suffering. In addition to natural causes, much suffering is due to immorality or the lack of integrity. And it is the plan of life for each of us to have the opportunity to be tested. We prove ourselves through some form of difficulty or suffering where we have to make a stand. Through our choices we eventually either make a stand for right—we're on the Lord's side—or we make a stand for wrong—we're on Satan's side. Actually, though often subtle to our thinking, we do the same thing we did in the pre-existence. While there, you and I chose good over evil. Here, we are given that choice another time, and once again, with eternal consequences.

My father once said to me, "It doesn't matter what happens to you. What matters is how you react to what happens to you." Will our choices draw us closer to the Lord or bitterly away?

Here we can't mince words, for ours is not an easy path. We are in a period of earth's history when many individuals are taking a stand with Satan. But *we have what it takes to stand for the right!* It is doable. It is expected. And each time we choose the right and turn to the Lord, we grow in strength, confidence, insight, and wisdom. Depending on our choices, the bad things that happen to us can confirm our faith as it shapes our lives for the better. We then become increasingly aware of who and what we are and less fearful and more effective in our service.

I'm reminded of a comment my youngest son, Tim, made one day some years ago when he was around fourteen years of age. We were talking about the frightening, hard times we experienced with a police order of protection in place, due to a pending divorce. He said to me, "It's not been so bad, Mom. I'd rather be a native trout any day." I asked him what he meant, and he told me how hatchery fish are hand-fed and consequently smaller and weaker than native fish. He said, "Native trout grow bigger, stronger, and smarter because they have to fight for everything they have."

Elder Orson F. Whitney said,

> No pain that we suffer, no trial that we experience is wasted. It ministers to our education, to the development of such qualities as patience, faith, fortitude, and humility. All that we suffer and all that we endure, especially when we endure it patiently, builds up our characters, purifies our hearts, expands our souls, and makes us more tender and charitable, more worthy to be called the children of God . . . and it is through sorrow and suffering, toil and tribulation, that we gain the education that we come here to acquire and which will make us more like our Father and Mother in heaven.[1]

We have what it takes to stand for the right! The Apostle Paul wrote, "There hath no temptation taken you but such as is common to man: but God is faithful, who will not suffer you to be tempted above that ye are able; but will with the temptation also make a way to escape, that ye may be able to bear it" (1 Corinthians 10:13). *We have the greater power, not Satan.*

We have a choice every minute of every day; the thoughts we form to determine those choices are what distinguish us for eternity. Before a choice is made, there is a thought, sometimes only flickering, but still a thought. As a woman thinketh, so is she. The challenge comes then not from without, but from

3

within—from our thoughts. Keeping our focus on the simple pattern presented in this book diminishes Satan's ability to play with and abuse our minds. There's nothing new about this pattern. It's been presented by the prophets for all time, but we're now in a place of extreme importance. The early pioneers stood strong in the period of the restoration of the gospel of Jesus Christ. We are what might be termed the modern-day pioneers. Our job is to stand strong in a period of worldly deterioration. No matter what our parents have done or do, no matter how we are treated by our husbands, no matter what choices our children make, our job is to stand steadfast and immovable in strict obedience, in total commitment, without (our actions) and within (our thoughts), standing on the Lord's side.

The stories and experiences included in this book are not presented to set myself or anyone else up as being better or more worthy than anyone else. They are presented as a witness of the truthfulness of the power and safety in this simple pattern the Lord gave us.

I've always loved the term "being carried in the hollow of His hand." Looking back through my most traumatic years, I can see now, and felt then, that I was being carried by the Lord.

Without a doubt there is great power in music. Good music—music that helps us feel the Lord by our sides—greatly influences our thoughts. Sometimes it's the actual words of a song; sometimes it's the melody; sometimes it's the beautiful memories of when or how it was sung. Music can make me feel like I can face my challenges with determination and accomplish what needs to be done. That's how Janice Kapp Perry's music helped me through some very difficult years. I had a tape of her music in my car. Wherever I traveled, I was influenced by her words and melodies. I can't say I had a favorite, but "In the Hollow of His Hand" was significant. I wanted, no, I needed desperately to be lifted up and carried by Him . . . I listened to that song over and over and over.

A few weeks ago, I was inspired by that song to write the following words. They aren't lyrics because they don't fit any music. They weren't written for song. They were written to express a simple pattern that if followed, always ends in a successful tapestry of life.

Dear Lord, please listen to my humble prayer,

And keep me always in Thy tender care.

As I prepare to meet the struggles of each day,

May I accept Thy will, listen, and obey.

Ever send Thy Spirit from above

To direct my footsteps with Thy love.

Teach me how to do my part;

Help me serve with all my heart.

May my understanding deepen and increase.

Let me know the special blessing of Thy peace.

Oh, keep me safe and bring me home again,

Thy precious daughter ever to remain.

Show me how to overcome my fears;

Comfort me and wipe away my tears.

Let me see what I might be

Fay A. Klingler

> *In my reaching for eternity.*
>
> *Give me courage to take a valiant stand*
>
> *And find shelter in the hollow of Thy hand.*

NOTE:

1. Orson F. Whitney, in Dennis D. Flake, *Orson F. Whitney's Philosophy of Education* (Provo: Brigham Young University, Department of Educational Leadership, 1989), 96.

CHAPTER 2

Identity

The Spirit itself beareth witness with our spirit, that we are the children of God: And if children, then heirs, heirs of God, and joint-heirs with Christ.
— Romans 8:16–17

One of my precious granddaughters, Ashlee, the day after her fourth birthday, was asked the following questions. Here are her responses.

> *What do you think it means to be a child of God?* "It means that we have to pray for Jesus."
> *Do you get any power from God?* "Yes, and I pray to Him."
> *Does God know what you are doing and how you feel?* "Yes, because He looks and He has eyes."
> *Will He help you when you feel bad?* "Yes."
> *Do you love Him?* "Yes."

Think about it. How would you answer those questions? What do you think it means to be a child of God? Do we get any power from God? Does God know what we are doing and

7

how we feel? Will He help us when we feel bad, or shall we say, when bad things happen to us? Do we love Him? And shall we ask another, "Does He love us?"

When I really thought about it, I became confused by what is meant from the term "I am a child of God," or "I am a daughter of God." It's in the Young Women theme—"We are daughters of our Heavenly Father." It's the opening line of the favorite song of thousands of Primary children—"I Am a Child of God." But the Relief Society declaration provides a word with considerable clarification—"We are beloved spirit daughters of God."

In the Pearl of Great Price we read,

> For I, the Lord God, had created all the children of men; . . . for in heaven created I them. . . . And I, the Lord God, formed man from the dust of the ground, and breathed into his nostrils the breath of life; and man became a living soul, the first flesh upon the earth, the first man also; nevertheless, all things were before created; but spiritually were they created and made according to my word. (Moses 3:5,7)

That same point is made in Teachings of Presidents of the Church: Joseph F. Smith. As we read it, we can plug the word woman in place of the word man, "Man [Woman], as a spirit, was begotten and born of heavenly parents and reared to maturity in the eternal mansions of the Father, prior to coming upon the earth in a temporal [physical] body,"[1]

It's clear then, as the Relief Society declaration states, that we are spirit daughters of our Heavenly Father. But if we are daughters of God, why is it written in the scriptures that we may *become* daughters of God?

> But verily, verily, I say unto you, that as many as receive me, to them will I give power to *become* the sons [daughters]

of God, even to them that believe on my name. (D&C 11:30; emphasis added)

I came unto mine own, and mine own received me not; but unto as many as received me gave I power to do many miracles, and to *become* the sons [and daughters] of God; and even unto them that believed on my name gave I power to obtain eternal life. (D&C 45:8; emphasis added)

And now, because of the covenant which ye have made ye *shall* be called the children of Christ, his sons, and his daughters: for behold, this day he hath spiritually begotten you; for ye say that your hearts are changed through faith on his name; therefore, ye are born of him and have become his sons and his daughters. (Mosiah 5:7; emphasis added)

Bruce R. McConkie's explanation helped me understand:

All women are the daughters of God because of their pre-existent birth as female spirits. However, the designation *daughters of God*, as used in the revelations, has a far more pointed meaning than this. Just as men who pursue a steadfast course toward exaltation become the sons of God while in this life, so women who walk hand-in-hand in obedience with them become the daughters of God.[2]

Therefore, God created my spirit and I became a spirit daughter of God. That title came free of charge, so to speak. But if I want Him to continue in the eternities to claim me as a daughter, I have to earn it. Every woman born on the earth was given the light of Christ—the ability to tell the difference between right and wrong—to help her on this journey of becoming. Every woman was sent on her way with another gift, that of agency—the power to obey or disobey and to progress according to individual choice. And to benefit His children who love Him and want to do His will, everyone was given at least one additional gift, such as wisdom, faith, or discernment, along with the promise that more could be had for the asking by those who were obedient (see D&C 46:8–33).

God made it clear, however, that this journey of becoming would not be easy, that woman's natural tendency would not be to lean on God and be obedient. To obtain the greatest gift of all, that of eternal life, through the clear use of choice, a woman has to follow the will or the desire of her Father in Heaven. And His will or desire is that she turn to Him for direction, no matter what happens, and act on the guidance she receives.

> For the natural man [woman] is an enemy to God, and has been from the fall of Adam, and will be, forever and ever, *unless* he [she] yields to the enticings of the Holy Spirit, and putteth off the natural man and becometh a saint through the atonement of Christ the Lord, and becometh as a child, submissive, meek, humble, patient, full of love, willing to submit to all things which the Lord seeth fit to inflict upon him [her], even as a child doth submit to his father. (Mosiah 3:19; emphasis added)

That thought brings me back to Doctrine and Covenants 45:8, mentioned earlier—"I came unto mine own, and mine own received me not; but unto as many as received me gave I power to do many miracles, and to become the sons [and daughters] of God; and even unto them that believed on my name gave I power to obtain eternal life"—the *power to become,* the *power to obtain.*

There we have it, the first thread of power and safety—recognizing our identity and acting with all our might to *become* daughters of God. And by grasping that thread, you and I and every woman born on the earth, regardless of our color, wealth, or age, can be led to safety and back into the arms of the Father.

I'm reminded of how an earthly father might prepare a written will to bequeath to his children what he possesses. It might go something like this. "I give to my daughter, Dawn, all my earthly possessions—my land, my home, my car, my money— everything I own." Sometimes the will even has a provision in it, stipulating the child must do something to receive the belongings. It might include a caveat: "everything I own . . . if she works for my company for a year," or ". . . if she gets her bachelor's degree." Then because of who she is—the father's daughter—if she follows the desire of the father stated in the will, she receives or inherits his possessions.

The scriptures might be compared to a written will. If a woman grasps that thread of power—turns to the Father and does what He says no matter what—and becomes a daughter of God, what does the Father promise to bequeath to her? In other words, what do the scriptures tell us we can claim or inherit if we become daughters of God? *We inherit the greatest gift of all— we have the right to claim eternal life.*

"If you keep my commandments and endure to the end you shall have *eternal life, which gift is the greatest of all the gifts of God*" (D&C 14:7; emphasis added).

And what is eternal life? Why is it such a great gift? It is overcoming all things, having all power, and subduing all enemies. It is living in the presence of God. It is living as God lives and continuing the family unit in eternity.

Here in the written will of our Father (not "will" in the case of death, but "will" in the case of desire)—the scriptures—we learn we can inherit everything (see D&C 76:50–70):

> And again we bear record—for we saw and heard, and this is the testimony of the gospel of Christ concerning them who shall come forth in the resurrection of the just—

They are they who received the testimony of Jesus, and believed on his name and were baptized after the manner of his burial, being buried in the water in his name, and this according to the commandment which he has given—

That by keeping the commandments they might be washed and cleansed from all their sins, and receive the Holy Spirit by the laying on of the hands of him who is ordained and sealed unto this power;

And who overcome by faith, and are sealed by the Holy Spirit of promise, which the Father sheds forth upon all those who are just and true.

They are they who are the church of the Firstborn.

They are they into whose hands the Father has given all things—

. . . Wherefore, as it is written, they are gods, even the sons [daughters] of God—

Wherefore, all things are theirs, whether life or death, or things present, or things to come, all are theirs and they are Christ's, and Christ is God's.

And they shall overcome all things.

Wherefore, let no man [woman] glory in man, but rather let him glory in God, who shall subdue all enemies under his feet.

These shall dwell in the presence of God and his Christ forever and ever.

These are they whom he shall bring with him, when he shall come in the clouds of heaven to reign on the earth over his people.

These are they who shall have part in the first resurrection.

These are they who shall come forth in the resurrection of the just.

These are they who are come unto Mount Zion, and unto the city of the living God, the heavenly place, the holiest of all.

. . . These are they whose names are written in heaven, where God and Christ are the judge of all.

These are they who are just men [women] made perfect through Jesus the mediator of the new covenant, who wrought out this perfect atonement through the shedding of his own blood.

These are they whose bodies are celestial, whose glory is that of the sun, even the glory of God, the highest of all, whose glory the sun of the firmament is written of as being typical.

The scriptures are clear. To claim our inheritance, we have to fulfill the stipulations of the will of God—make choices in keeping with His desire and direction. We must be baptized, receive the Holy Ghost, keep the commandments, live by faith, lean on God, and give thanks and recognition to Him.

He does not leave us stranded here to accomplish all that. As we strive to be worthy, we are entitled to personal revelation. And no matter where, when, or under what circumstances we live, so long as our hands, hearts, and minds are clean and pure, the unlimited power in the priesthood can aid us in our journey. As women, we do not have the authority to hold the priesthood nor do we have the authority to administer in priesthood ordinances, but we do have the right to enjoy the blessings of the priesthood given by those who are ordained with that authority.

One of the responsibilities I had while serving on the Church Hosting Board was to prepare "Memorable Moments" for distribution to the 1,200 or so hosting missionaries on Temple Square. "Memorable Moments" were descriptions of special experiences the missionaries wanted to share with each other. I was so impressed by the "Memorable Moment" given to me by Margie Stephenson, who was serving in the Church Office Building, that I asked her permission to share it here with you.

I was serving at the west desk on the 26th floor when a tour stopped at the Guest Register to sign their names. Two of the people in the group were speaking Spanish. So I said something to them in Spanish and we struck up a conversation. They were two counselors in a branch in Texas here for Conference. One was from Texas and one was an older man from Mexico.

As they signed their names, one turned to the other and asked him to finish filling out his information. He then turned to me and said, "I didn't learn to read and write until I was 43." He proceeded to tell me his story.

He told me the stake president called him to be the bishop of his ward. He told his leaders he couldn't be bishop because he couldn't read or write. The stake president said, "Adam didn't have schools to teach him to read or write. How did he learn?"

"Of course God taught him."

"Then why can't God teach you?"

The stake president told him he was going to give him a blessing and within ten days or so he would be able to begin reading. The blessing was given and this man said that within seconds of the blessing being finished, he opened his eyes and looked at a book that was sitting close by. He could read! He said from that moment until today he has been able to read and write.

The other thing this sweet, humble man said before he left was, "You sisters don't understand what a blessing you have to be able to serve here. You are working in God's kingdom!"

I was very humbled at the testimony and faith of this sweet man from Mexico.

The power of the priesthood is real. Later I will tell you of one of my own miraculous dealings with that great power. But for now let me mention just one marvelous blessing available to us through the power of the priesthood—a patriarchal blessing.

I have a great deal of admiration for ordained stake patriarchs. It can be exhausting work to put your life and mind in order to provide prophetic insight. The blessings they give are more than just guides or road maps. A patriarchal blessing can offer strength to the recipient and be a shield and a protection. Our patriarchal blessings are very personal treasures dictated by the Spirit. An essential part of those blessings is the declaration of our lineage. Yes, beyond being spirit daughters of God!

In addition to our lineage, through the Spirit, the patriarch names some of the blessings and promises we are entitled to, depending on our faithfulness. Our patriarchal blessings might also provide specific warnings and admonitions the patriarch is prompted to give for the accomplishment of our life's missions. The realization of all the promised blessings is, of course, conditional. Just as it is in claiming our inheritance as daughters of God, we must fulfill the stipulations of the will of God—make choices in keeping with His desire and direction. Depending on our choices, we can choose to forfeit those blessings and take a different route, or we can choose to carefully follow the road map and watch as each blessing unfolds. With the prerequisite of faithfulness, those blessings will happen in the Lord's due time, not always the timetable we wish for. But because He is bound when we do what He says, with patience all blessings come to pass.

In February 2011, Sister Elaine S. Dalton, President of the General Young Women Presidency, spoke at a conference in California to more than 1,000 young women. As she offered the closing remarks, she shared the sacredness of when she received her patriarchal blessing at age fourteen. She said that her blessing stated she would travel the earth to bear testimony of the gospel, and she realized she was living that prophecy. She testified that the Lord intimately knows each of us. If the Lord knew her, as a shy 14-year-old girl, then surely He knows you and He knows me.

God and His Beloved Son have all power to bless us. They have all knowledge about us. Luke, the physician, puts our value into perspective. "Are not five sparrows sold for two farthings, and not one of them is forgotten before God? *But even the very hairs of your head are all numbered. Fear not therefore: ye are of more value than many sparrows*" (Luke 12:6–7; emphasis added).

Luke also points out God's patience and individual love for us with two intermingled stories. He tells of a time when a man named Jairus requested that Jesus come home with him and bless his only daughter, who was dying. On their way, many people crowded around Jesus and He felt someone touch Him, and He stopped and asked, "Who touched me?"

Can you imagine how Jairus felt? Here he's in a rush to save his daughter's life and Jesus seems to get side-tracked. And what about the woman who touched Jesus? It can't have been easy for her either—to have pressed her way through the crowd. She might have been thinking, *"Who am I that He would heal me? I won't bother Him. I'll just touch His robe. That's all I need. If I can just touch His robe, I'll be better."*

Peter, who is traveling with Jesus, is astonished and says, "Master, the multitude throng thee and press thee, and sayest thou, Who touched me?" And Jesus said, "Somebody hath touched me: for I perceive that virtue is gone out of me" (Luke 8:45–46).

So out of the whole crowd Jesus is aware of this one woman in particular who touched Him and was healed immediately— this humble one who trusted Him, who had faith that He could help her. He turned to her and said, "Daughter, be of good comfort: thy faith hath made thee whole; go in peace" (Luke 8:48).

Then came the blow to Jairus. Before Jesus even finished speaking to the woman, a runner came from Jairus's house, saying to him, "Thy daughter is dead; trouble not the Master" (Luke 8:49).

Jairus might have thought, *"What? He stops to help this woman, and in the meantime my daughter dies?"*

But then Jesus quickly gives him hope again by responding to the runner, "Fear not: believe only, and she shall be made whole" (Luke 8:50).

We can assume the crowd followed. Who wouldn't, hearing a statement like that from the Master? But Jesus only allowed the parents, Peter, James, and John to go in. He put all others out of the house. Why? They did not follow because they believed Him. It was as though they followed to catch Him in error or to be entertained, for they laughed him to scorn. They did not understand nor trust His power. "And he put them all out, and took her by the hand, and called, saying, Maid, arise. And her spirit came again, and she arose straightway: and he commanded to give her meat" (Luke 8:54–55).

Jesus had compassion on the woman who in faith touched his robe. Jairus, too, must have had great faith to have sought after Jesus, believing He could heal his daughter. Then, even seeing disappointment in Jairus's eyes at the runner's news, Jesus cared for the girl and brought her back to life.

"Fear not: believe only," He said. His extreme compassion and power are also there for you and me. As we exercise our faith, we can witness miracles taking place all through our lives. Throughout the remainder of this book is one example after another of just such a witness. We must have complete confidence that He knows us and cares about us personally, individually.

I once lived in the Chicago, Illinois, area. My move west was overwhelmingly eventful. Each day our experiences could have ended in tragedy. We experienced a driver falling asleep at the wheel, getting lost, a flat tire on a fully-packed truck in the middle of nowhere, and being robbed. I kept a little log of the events as we traveled. In my new ward in Arizona, I was asked to speak in sacrament meeting. I had the distinct impression I should find that log and talk about the faith we had to exercise as we worked through each challenge. But I couldn't find the log. Running out of time, I searched through every box, cupboard, and shelf, but still could not locate the log. I remember standing in my bedroom, frustrated and thinking to myself, *"If you'd just take the time to kneel down and ask, He would show you where it is."* I no more than had that thought and I was directed to a shelf, picked up a stack of papers (that I had already looked through multiple times), and simply lifted the log from its hiding place. I immediately got on my knees and thanked my Heavenly Father for answering my prayer, even in my weakness when I did not take the time to ask appropriately.

The Lord knows our names. He knows our thoughts. He knows our circumstances. He hears our prayers and wants to bless us in every righteous desire of our hearts. Even if we can't see it now, as we obey Heavenly Father, we can trust that He will put us in places or situations in our lives that will prove to help us in the future.

If we are concerned about worthiness, we can remember this gift, too, that we were given—the Atonement. Repentance makes it possible for us to make course corrections and find the loving, caring embrace of the Savior. As stated by Nephi, we learn through life's experiences precept upon precept:

> For behold, thus saith the Lord God: I will give unto the children of men line upon line, precept upon precept, here a little and there a little; and blessed are those who hearken unto my precepts, and lend an ear unto my counsel, for they shall learn wisdom; for unto him that receiveth I will give more; and from them that shall say, we have enough, from them shall be taken away even that which they have. (2 Nephi 28:30)

As long as we work to keep our focus on doing what is right and becoming daughters of God, and put in our best efforts, even in our weakness, the Lord will lift us up, give us strength, and point us again in the right direction. Remember, if we choose it to be so, our power is greater than the tempter's.

People who see mistakes as opportunities for learning can keep going as challenges appear. We can use mistakes as evidence that we should search for information, not that we should give up. I don't know where it came from, but I've had this little saying that I've carried with me from one move to the next—"We are continually faced by great opportunities brilliantly disguised as insoluble problems."

When we are faced with hard times, we can avoid the temptation to say to ourselves, "I can't do this. I give up." We must not question whether or not we can handle it. Just ask ourselves, "*How* am I going to handle it?" We can use our ingenuity and start looking for options and solutions to resolve our challenges.

It is amazing how much more we can handle than we believe we can. Honestly, we have tremendous reserves we're not even aware of. Our creative abilities will grow as we recognize new avenues to achieve our ambitions. We can reevaluate where we're headed and how we want to get there. Determine where we are now. What went right? What went wrong? Why? Pat ourselves on the back for trying. We can then begin to feel a sense of satisfaction not just for those workable parts that go well and are accomplished, but for the times we tried, even if it didn't work. The act of trying, or the act of getting back up and trying *again*, is an accomplishment to be applauded.

As we work to become daughters of God, we are entitled to answers and directions from a loving God. I know He loves me and I know He loves you. We must have hope in our future and move forward with a calm assurance that we are not alone.

Because we know who we are, we must act accordingly. There are certain things we can never do, certain thoughts we can never entertain. Because they are not worthy of who we are, there are certain places we can never go.

We love God and express thanks for the opportunity to participate in His plan. We avoid any identity crisis because we understand and embrace our female gender and role, and we reverence life. Without allowing peers to make our choices, as daughters of God, we reflect that for which we seek by dressing modestly with skirts low enough and blouses high enough. We choose to affiliate with people who bring us closer to God and share our values. We use clean and intelligent language that uplifts, encourages, and compliments others. We keep the Sabbath day holy. We treat our bodies as sacred temples, which they are, and reserve sexual intimacy for marriage. We obey the law of tithing and look to the Savior as our example in serving others. We magnify and share our talents. As daughters of heavenly parents, we set a standard of excellence and integrity, increase our spiritual heritage, and set an example for all the world.

Now that I clearly know who I am and who I want to become, the questions posed to my young granddaughter Ashlee seem much easier to answer with confidence. What do you think it means to be a child of God? Do you get any power from God? Does God know what you are doing and how you feel? Will He help you when you feel bad? Do you love Him?

As we learn from the Young Women theme and the Relief Society declaration, to be, or become, a child of God—a daughter of God—we stand as witnesses of God at all times, wherever we may be. We act in faith, virtue, and integrity. We choose to make and keep sacred covenants, dedicate ourselves to strengthening home and family, delight in service, and find joy in womanhood.

Yes, definitely, we get power from God. And as we seek spiritual strength by following the promptings of the Holy Ghost, we gain confidence that Heavenly Father will not only guide us on the right path, but after we have done all we can He will open the necessary doors, allowing us to fulfill our humble goals to become rightful heirs.

Does God know what you are doing and how you feel? Will He help you when you feel bad? Absolutely! He knows us even better than we know ourselves. He loves us and wants us to be happy, to understand our divine destiny, and to succeed in striving for exaltation.

Do you love Him? Now that is really the clarifying question. If we love God, we show it by our faith, by our choices, by our actions, and by our truly devoted commitment to *become daughters of God!*

"Live up to the great and magnificent inheritance which the Lord God, your Father in Heaven, has provided for you," said President Gordon B. Hinckley. "Rise above the dust of the world. Know that you are daughters of God, children with a divine birthright. Walk in the sun with your heads high, knowing that you are loved and honored, that you are a part of his kingdom, and that there is for you a great work to be done which cannot be left to others." [3]

NOTES:

1. Joseph F. Smith, in *Teachings of Presidents of the Church: Joseph F. Smith* (Salt Lake City: The Church of Jesus Christ of Latter-day Saints, 1998), 335.

2. Bruce R. McConkie, *Mormon Doctrine* (Salt Lake City: Bookcraft, 1966), 179–180.

3. President Gordon B. Hinckley, "Live Up to Your Inheritance," *Ensign*, Nov. 1983, 84.

CHAPTER 3

Prayer

❧

Fear thou not; for I am with thee: be not dismayed; for I am thy God: I will
strengthen thee; yea, I will help thee; yea, I will uphold thee with the right
hand of my righteousness. . . . For I the Lord thy God will hold thy right
hand, saying unto thee, Fear not; I will help thee.
—Isaiah 41:10, 13

❧

W hen I was told I was going to be released from the Church
Hosting Board, I experienced a few weeks of sorrow,
feelings like grief. I was in mourning at the thought of not being
involved with the wonderful Church Hosting directors. I was
going to miss the Spirit that accompanied me when fulfilling
my duties, and I felt displaced. Then I received a "Memorable Moment" to prepare for a sister missionary. Her opening
remarks expressed her feelings of distress at the time her children grew up and moved out of the home—the empty nest. She
expressed the same type of feelings I had going through my
mind at the pending release from the Church Hosting Board,

and I began to realize how foolish we women can be when we focus our identity on anything but becoming a daughter of God. I'm not discounting that we should focus our efforts on being the best possible mothers, or the best teachers, or the best friends, daughters, sisters, grandmothers . . . But our identity—who and what we are, the foundation we work from in making decisions and facing life—must not be based on any title or season in life. How we choose to face life must be based on our relationship with our Heavenly Father as His spirit daughters and on working to become His heirs. That is the basis for our earthly experience and that is what gives us the power to find happiness and joy through eternity.

As in any loving relationship, communication is available between Heavenly Father and His daughters. He knows what we are doing, what we are feeling, and what we are thinking. And He expects us to reason things out and decide our own path. The beauty of it is that with the gift of choice comes divine guidance just for the asking. Well, no, not always "just for the asking." After all, what kind of parent would give his child everything he or she asked for, especially if the parent knew it wouldn't be in the best interest of the child (or in the best interest of those associated with the child)?

Susanna McMahon, in her book *The Portable Therapist*, explains that good communication involves both problem-solving and supportive skills. Problem-solving communication is when someone talks about something and the other person gives feedback—advice not necessarily asked for

With supportive communication "you do not give advice unless you are specifically asked to do so," says Susanna. "Supportive communication means allowing the other person to feel good about solving the problem. . . . It means allowing the other [person] to say everything they want to say without interruptions or arguments. Supportive conversation first involves effective listening. . . . Support means that the other [person] knows you are there with them and that you will listen."[1] Heavenly Father uses supportive communication far more often than problem-solving communication.

In other words, Heavenly Father is there to give us advice *when we seek it.* But first, He wants us to grow by trying to figure things out for ourselves. This concept is made clear in Doctrine and Covenants 9:7–8: "Behold, you have not understood; you have supposed that I would give it unto you, when you took no thought save it was to ask me. But, behold, I say unto you, that you must study it out in your mind."

One excellent example of Heavenly Father's communication methods is given in the Book of Mormon. According to the instructions of the Lord, the brother of Jared and his brethren built eight barges to carry them across the sea. The barges were airtight. The brother of Jared prayed to the Lord, saying,

> O Lord, I have performed the work which thou hast commanded me, and I have made the barges according as thou hast directed me. And behold, O Lord, in them there is no light; whither shall we steer? And also we shall perish, for in them we cannot breathe, save it is the air which is in them; therefore we shall perish. (Ether 2:18–19)

Note the pattern here. The brother of Jared asked the Lord for advice. In this case, the Lord did not say to the brother of Jared, "When you've got those boats made, there won't be enough light or air in them. So you've got to do this . . ." No, He waited for the brother of Jared to figure it out and ask how to handle the problem.

The Lord gave him the answer to one of his questions.

> And the Lord said unto the brother of Jared: Behold, thou shalt make a hole in the top, and also in the bottom; and when thou shalt suffer for air thou shalt unstop the hole and

receive air. And if it be so that the water come in upon thee, behold, ye shall stop the hole, that ye may not perish in the flood. (Ether 2:20)

And the brother of Jared followed the instructions and did as the Lord said. But what about the matter of no light?

The brother of Jared approached the Lord again, complaining about no light in the vessels. And the Lord asked him to suggest a solution. In the process, the Lord explained the limitations and expressed His complete support.

For behold, ye cannot have windows, for they will be dashed in pieces; neither shall ye take fire with you, for ye shall not go by the light of fire. For behold, ye shall be as a whale in the midst of the sea; for the mountain waves shall dash upon you. Nevertheless, I will bring you up again out of the depths of the sea; for the winds have gone forth out of my mouth, and also the rains and the floods have I sent forth. And behold, I prepare you against these things; for ye cannot cross this great deep save I prepare you against the waves of the sea, and the winds which have gone forth, and the floods which shall come. Therefore what will ye that I should prepare for you that ye may have light when ye are swallowed up in the depths of the sea? (Ether 2:23–25)

So the brother of Jared thought it through and came up with an idea. He went on the mountain and melted down a rock to produce sixteen small stones. The stones were white and clear, like transparent glass. He went to the top of the mountain and prayed again to the Lord, saying,

O Lord, thou hast said that we must be encompassed about by the floods. Now behold, O Lord, and do not be angry with thy servant because of his weakness before thee. . . . O Lord, thou hast given us a commandment that we must call upon thee, that from thee we may receive according to our desires. . . . O Lord, look upon me in pity, and turn away thine anger from this thy people, and suffer not that they shall go forth across this raging deep in darkness; but behold these things which I have molten out of the rock. And I know, O Lord, that thou hast all power, and can do whatsoever thou wilt for the benefit of man; therefore touch these stones, O Lord, with thy finger, and prepare them that they may shine forth in darkness; and they shall shine forth unto us in the vessels which we have prepared, that we may have light while we shall cross the sea. (Ether 3:2–4)

Because of his great faith, the Lord not only touched each stone with His finger, giving them illumination, but the brother of Jared was allowed to see the Lord's finger and then His whole spirit body. And this was not all. Because the brother of Jared had trust in the Lord's power and faith that his requests would be granted, he was rewarded with knowledge and the Lord ministered unto him.

Here in the story we get a glimpse of the profound choreography of the Lord. He directs the brother of Jared not to tell others about his experience, but to write it down. The Lord further explains that He will confound the language of the writing so no one can interpret it. He gives him two stones and tells the brother of Jared to seal the stones up with the writing. All this, planned so many years ahead, so that those stones—those interpreters—could be used to translate writings for the benefit of future generations.

Let's go back just a minute to complete the blueprint presented in Doctrine and Covenants section 9, mentioned earlier. The Lord said our part included reasoning it out in our minds and asking Him if the conclusion we've come to is correct or right. Then He gives a promise, "if it is right I will cause that your bosom shall burn within you; therefore, you shall feel that it is right. But if it be not right you shall have no such feelings, but you shall have a stupor of thought that shall cause you to forget the thing which is wrong" (D&C 9:8–9).

So in order to keep this precious line of communication open we must:

- Look for solutions to our problem(s) by reasoning it out in our minds

- Want to talk to Heavenly Father to receive advice or comfort

- Ask in specific terms for the desired advice or comfort

- Listen for the answer(s)

- Act upon the advice given

If all our needs were met without hesitation and without effort on our part, how would we learn? How would we grow or become stronger? At one of my visits to the Museum of Science and Industry in Chicago, Illinois, I was inspired by the work and determination prominent in one of the exhibits—a large incubator containing fertile chicken eggs and a few newly hatched chicks. I stood by and watched a chick struggle as it worked its way through the shell of the egg and flop to the incubator floor in exhaustion. It lay there wet for some time, every ounce of energy spent except that for breathing. Gradually it began to move and very slowly dried. In time it stood, peeping its delight to be alive and began working to find something to eat!

By the nineteenth day of incubation, a chick is too big to get enough oxygen through the pores in the eggshell. It must do something or die. At the flat end of the egg is an air sack. By this time, a small egg-tooth has grown onto the beak of the chick. It uses this little tooth to peck a hole into the air sack. The air sack provides just six hours of air for the chick to breathe before breaking through the shell. The chick's fight for freedom from the egg, though exhausting, builds necessary muscles. Its determined passion to crack open the egg results in adequate amounts of outside air to sustain life.

Like for the chicken, solutions to our problems are available. Remember, Heavenly Father is in charge. He plans ahead. He does not put more trouble in our path than we can handle. But for us to grow our spiritual muscles and gain adequate insight—spiritual air—to see us through life's hardships, we have to do our part to chip away the eggshell, or fight to find solutions to our problems. Oh yes, once we seek it, sometimes we identify the solutions as they come in obvious, miraculous ways, or they come in the form of knowledge through apparent revelation. But more often they come in simple ways, like a word or a sentence in a conversation with a friend, or from reading something. We may be seeking an answer to a problem and find the solution in something the Sunday School teacher presents in her lesson—maybe not the whole answer, but a piece. Just like little chips in the eggshell eventually open the way for the chick, when we focus on finding solutions, a way opens for us to solve our problems.

At times, we may be asking for divine assistance and wonder if we're being heard because we don't readily get an answer we identify. Heavenly Father listens to us unconditionally. Whether we're happy or sad or grateful or mad, He always listens. That's a skill of a good communicator. But too many of us have not developed the skill of effective listening. We're too busy talking!

When my children were young, I had a poster magnetized to the refrigerator in the kitchen. Printed on it were the following listening rules:

1. Look at person speaking

2. Listen with ears and brain

3. Keep hands and feet to self

4. Mouth is quiet

Regarding answer to prayer, if we practice listening—really listening—we concentrate on hearing or feeling what the Lord tells us rather than on what we want to hear or want to say. And we are patient, knowing the answer will come, but in the time-table of the Lord, since He sees the whole picture and we only see a puzzle piece at a time. While in distress, it may be difficult to stop our asking and concentrate on listening, but effective listening is essential to receiving comfort and guidance from the Lord.

To further show His support, the Lord gave us the precious gift of the Holy Ghost. When we are baptized and are obedient, we are blessed with the constant companionship of the Holy Ghost. What is the job or commission of the Holy Ghost? The Holy Ghost is given to:

- Testify of the Divine Sonship of Jesus Christ

- Help us to know and understand things that are true

- Offer a voice of warning to protect us from spiritual or physical danger or temptation

- Enlighten our minds—sharpen our discernment to judge wisely

- Speak peace

- Lead us to do good

- Provide comfort during times of trial, pain, or sorrow

In a classic statement, Elder Parley P. Pratt describes the refining and perfecting power of the Holy Ghost:

The gift of the Holy Ghost . . . quickens all the intellectual faculties, increases, enlarges, expands, and purifies all the natural passions and affections, and adapts them, by the gift of wisdom, to their lawful use. It inspires, develops, cultivates, and matures all the fine-toned sympathies, joys, tastes, kindred feelings, and affections of our nature. It inspires virtue, kindness, goodness, tenderness, gentleness, and charity. It develops beauty of person, form, and features. It tends to health, vigor, animation, and social feeling. It invigorates all the faculties of the physical and intellectual man. It strengthens and gives tone to the nerves. In short, it is, as it were, marrow to the bone, joy to the heart, light to the eyes, music to the ears, and life to the whole being.[2]

Wow, what a gift! And all we need to do to have the companionship of the Holy Ghost is to turn our hearts to God and give our best efforts in becoming His heirs.

Elder LeGrand Richards made this statement:

I would rather have my children and my children's children enjoy the companionship of the Holy Ghost than any other companionship in this world because if they will heed the promptings of that Spirit, he will lead them into all truth and see them safely back into the presence of their Father in heaven.[3]

My cousin Brookie Dickerson experienced tragedy when her son committed suicide. As is her habit, she leaned on the Lord for support. Some years later she said, "There were only two who really knew my heartache when our son died—Heavenly Father and His Son. And They sent the Holy Ghost to build a protective shield around me. I have never felt the power of the Atonement as I did during that time."

I love that phrase—"a protective shield." She said it was

a feeling of security like being encompassed in a cocoon and bathed in the warmth of Heavenly Father's love.

President Boyd K. Packer explained the influence of the Holy Ghost as a gentle prompting that tells us what to do or what to say, or it may caution or warn us. President Packer said the Holy Ghost speaks with a voice that we feel more than we hear.

When I was in the process of writing *Shattered: Six Steps from Betrayal to Recovery*, I had a remarkable experience with quiet communication from the Holy Ghost. At one point, I couldn't figure out what to write. I knelt and prayed for help. I so wanted to convey what the Lord would have in that book. At the conclusion of my prayer, I sat at my computer with my fingers on the keys, waiting for an answer. I waited for what seemed a long time before thoughts came into my mind. I thought, *"But this doesn't make any sense. It doesn't fit anything I've written."* After a few minutes, I knelt again in prayer with the same request as before. And again, when I sat at my computer, the same thoughts and feelings flooded my mind and I said, *"I don't understand. How does this fit?"* Now, I know memory can play tricks with you, but as I remember it, I repeated the process once again before I heard a definite but quiet voice in my mind say, *"If you're going to ask for revelation, don't you think you ought to write it down?"*

I was startled, and quickly moved the keys to type what I had been told. More words came then, and I realized how they all fit together, not only for that chapter, but the next.

That example brings us to the "doing" part of prayer, or acting upon the advice given. Remember the story of the brother of Jared and how air was obtained for the voyage in the barges? The Lord told the brother of Jared to make a hole in the top and also in the bottom of each boat. When the people needed air, they simply had to unstop a hole and receive it. We don't know whether the brother of Jared made the holes himself or directed others to make the holes, but we do know the directions of the Lord were followed—the doing was accomplished.

After *Shattered: Six Steps from Betrayal to Recovery* was published, I was invited to speak in Arizona in conjunction with their state's Coalition Against Domestic Violence. As an introduction, I was to be on morning television, then give my presentation in the evening. A newspaper article preceded my trip. After the article was released, I received a phone call from an individual working at the bookstore sponsoring the event. The person said, "We've just received a threatening call against you if you come to speak. We've already contacted the police. They asked us to find out if you know who might want to hurt you." She went on to ask for names and pictures of individuals the police should be looking for.

The individual was obviously very excited; her words came rapidly. She sounded scared. I was shocked and didn't immediately respond. So she repeated herself. At that, I said I didn't have any idea who would want to hurt me, and that I'd have to get back to her.

At that time I worked in my husband's company and was sitting at my office desk. I don't remember exactly what happened next, but I remember going in tears to my husband's office, explaining what I had been told. He immediately said we needed to cancel the event. I said I didn't want to do that because too much work had been put into organizing the event, and canceling would affect too many people.

During the next 24 hours, I prayed to know what to do and a calmness came over me. I was able to think rationally. I thought of my favorite scripture found in 2 Timothy 1:7—"For God hath not given us the spirit of fear; but of power, and of love, and of a sound mind." I was directed to read my patriarchal blessing where there is a significant statement regarding my safety, and I decided to lean on the power of faith and put myself "in the hollow of His hand."

I called the bookstore back and asked to speak directly to the individual who received the threat. I asked him, "What exactly did the caller say?" I gave the information I received to one of our sons who, at one time, worked for an armored car company. He still owned a bulletproof vest and suggested I wear it. So it was decided, for my protection, I would wear the vest, and a plain-clothed policeman would patrol the event.

As you can imagine, I had some anxiety. I knew my husband and family were worried, too, but honestly, in my mind I knew I would be okay because I felt that assurance from the Lord. And I was; I was fine. I wore that heavy, hot vest (remember, I was in Arizona!) all through the event. At the conclusion, when individuals lined up to have me sign books, I needed some cooling air and opened my jacket, revealing the vest over my blouse. Most of the people there had come to learn how to be safe in betrayal situations. Many experienced violence and fear every day. So when they saw the vest, I heard audible gasps. I quickly explained I was fine and just needed some air. I went ahead and took off the vest. They hovered around me, demanding that I put the vest back on before leaving the building, and I promised I would. I actually felt sorry for them because they didn't know what I knew—that I would be protected even without the vest. They couldn't see the shield I wore under the vest. It was my shield of faith and trust—*far more powerful than any man made device.* This was the shield I did not dare remove!

For me, the doing part of prayer in this situation was to embrace the peace and comfort provided by the Holy Ghost. Feeling the assurance that I would be safe made it possible for me to deliver my message and give hope to those who attended.

Prayer—communication with the Lord—and the resulting promptings from the Spirit act like a lifeguard, pulling us in to safety. When we reverence our divine identity, we overcome the natural woman and turn to God for our guidance, comfort, and support. We listen with keen sensitivity to the Spirit with our minds and hearts to hear the answers. Sometimes that means, with awareness, we move forward with our plans. Other times it means, without hesitation, we must have the courage to stand up and walk away from dangerous situations.

We are placed here on earth at a time when we must never underestimate or undervalue our divine role as powerful women—daughters of God. We are the everyday instruments God uses to do His work. Only the adversary would have us believe otherwise. Remember, we can *always* call upon our Father for assistance. Unless by our own choice, we are *never* left alone. If we grasp His unfailing love and do our part to receive the sweet influence and companionship of the Holy Ghost, we will find our way safely through our most difficult experiences and recognize answers to our earnest prayers. This love and help is offered to every woman who seeks it, no matter her age, race, or socioeconomic circumstance.

In a farewell speech to his home state in Springfield, Illinois, as he left for Washington, DC, newly elected President Abraham Lincoln said, "I now leave, not knowing when or whether ever I may return, with a task before me greater than that which rested upon Washington. Without the assistance of that Divine Being who ever attended him, I cannot succeed. *With the assistance I cannot fail*" (emphasis added).[4]

With God's assistance *we* cannot fail!

As we lean on God and trust Him, we receive revelation to guide us in the simple things as well as the big things. Recently, my cousin Brookie was asked to speak in stake conference.

After she spoke, I asked her how it went and she wrote to me the following:

> I got some very positive feedback. I felt good about it. My constant prayer through the preparation was, "Heavenly Father, you know who will be there. You know what they need. Please help me say what would help at least one sister."

> After the conference, a sister came up to me with tears in her eyes and said, "I brought a sister with me today and you said exactly what she needed to hear. Thank you." So, as usual, Heavenly Father answered my prayer and was loving enough to *let me know* He'd answered it. Isn't He amazing! I love Him so much.

Sometimes those answers come easily. Other times it seems painfully difficult.

We've all probably read or heard about Enos and his wrestle with God. Enos was taught the joy of eternal life by his father. One day as he was hunting in the forest, he pondered on those teachings and knelt to pray.

> And I will tell you of the wrestle which I had before God, before I received a remission of my sins. . .

> And my soul hungered; and I kneeled down before my Maker, and I cried unto him in mighty prayer and supplication for mine own soul; and all the day long did I cry unto him; yea, and when the night came I did still raise my voice high that it reached the heavens. And there came a voice unto me, saying: Enos, thy sins are forgiven thee, and thou shalt be blessed. And I, Enos, knew that God could not lie, wherefore, my guilt was swept away. And I said: Lord, how is it done? And he said unto me: Because of thy faith in Christ, whom thou hast never before heard nor seen. And many years pass away before he shall manifest himself in the flesh; wherefore, go to, thy faith hath made thee whole. (Enos 2, 4–8)

Note Enos's words: "and all the day long did I cry unto him; yea, and when the night came I did still raise my voice." This was no short prayer—he prayed all day and all night before the answer came. The word he used, "wrestle," can mean many things. In this case, I believe it means that he continued without ceasing to plead with the Lord for an answer to his prayer, and when the answer didn't come readily, he continued to plead with the Lord.

How easy it is to forget we've been heard and have received answers to our prayers in the past. When confronted with new problems or questions, and the solutions or answers don't come easily, we must not lose faith and hope. Bad things do happen to good people. We are all victims at one time or another when our personal world is in chaos. But we can also all be survivors when we choose to turn to the Lord. By continuing to "wrestle" with the Lord for answers and direction, we turn away bitterness and grow in character, hope, and faith.

In 2000, I interviewed Naomi W. Randall (now deceased). She was the author of the beloved song "I Am a Child of God." At that time, she was a widow and 92 years old. Here in her own words are the answers to my questions, which I feel are very fitting to the point I want to make that we don't give up, that we continue, over a lifetime, to "wrestle" with the Lord.

Question: As you have experienced it, how have you coped with life-changing disappointment or tragedy? What have your strategies been to pick yourself up and move on?

Answer: I put my faith and trust in the Lord. I relied on him to guide me. In addition, I would take each day at a time, but kept busy. I turned to family and friends and found that trying to be creative and do useful activities helped.

When I was recovering from major surgery, I turned to doing needlepoint, being creative and busy while I let my body heal. I did further handwork after my husband, Earl, died. I made special temple gifts for my family and friends. Doing for and thinking of others helped me with my personal hurt, but relying on the Lord helped the deeper hurt.

Question: Will you share a personal experience when you had to rely on your faith in Heavenly Father to lift you up after experiencing tragedy?

Answer: A personal experience after tragedy came one day in a chapel service shortly after Earl died. The song lyrics that I had composed, "I Am a Child of God," were being sung. I began to cry. Then I sobbed very hard. I got up and left the chapel to be by myself. The sobbing helped me release the hurt and get it out in the open where I could face it; then I could rely on the Lord and know He loved me and that He would look after me.

Question: When you experience tragedy, how do you get rid of the anger or the "why me?" feelings?

Answer: How I felt and got rid of the anger after a tragedy is in this example. I was irrigating the strawberries, again after my husband passed away. Earl and I had maintained a very large and beautiful yard; now I was trying to keep it up by myself. The water dam I had made broke and the water got away and ran all over the garden, causing big problems. I looked up and yelled, "Earl, I know I am not doing this very well, but you left me and I'm doing the best I can." Then I cried to the Lord, "You took him away from me and you'll have to help me." I wanted to express it and forget it. Expressing it out loud calmed my down, and I found the relief I needed. By getting it out of my system, I could then move on. Later I could even laugh at the experience.

Question: Is there a scripture that helps you through difficult times?

Answer: In my 28 years of service on the Primary General Board, as board member and in the Primary General Presidency, I very frequently relied on the following scriptures. Reviewing and reciting them in my mind gave me strength to press on and complete my assignments and work. The following two scriptures came especially strong to me when I was called to the Primary General Board of the Church, and as I was contemplating accepting this significant call to serve the entire Church.

The scripture in 1 Nephi 3:7 where Nephi's father sent him on a mission to go into Jerusalem to obtain the plates of brass that Laban had refused to give up. The young Nephi said unto his father, "I will go and do the things which the Lord hath commanded, for I know that the Lord giveth no commandments unto the children of men, save he shall prepare a way for them that they may accomplish the thing which he commandeth them."

Another is Proverbs 3:5–6, "Trust in the Lord with all thine heart; and lean not unto thine own understanding. In all thy ways acknowledge him, and he shall direct thy paths."

Question: How do you overcome your fears?

Answer: To overcome fear, I pray and have faith that things will turn out all right.

When considering how to overcome fear, I wrote the lyrics to a song titled "When Faith Endures" that goes like this:

I will not doubt, I will not fear;

God's love and strength are always near.

His promised gift helps me to find

An inner strength and peace of mind.

I give the Father willingly

My trust, my prayers, humility.

His spirit guides, his love assures

That fear departs when faith endures.

Later I added these words as a second verse:

When trials come, as come they will,

I'll try the more to do His will.

I'll pray for strength and courage strong,

And strive at length to right the wrong.

I'll cling to hope, give charity,

Reach out to those in need of me.

Pure love of Christ to me assures,

That burdens lift when faith endures.

(This hymn appears as Hymn 128 in the LDS hymnbook.)

Through all time, women have called upon God in prayer. When they remember they are daughters of God, prayer becomes natural and instinctive. According to the Bible dictionary, "prayer is the act by which the will of the Father and the will of the child are brought into correspondence with each other. The object of prayer is not to change the will of God, but to secure for ourselves and for others blessings that God is already willing to grant, but that are made conditional on our asking for them. Blessings require some work or effort on our part before we can obtain them. Prayer is a form of work, and is an appointed means for obtaining the highest of all blessings."

The scriptures give us the proper order for prayer:

1. We address our Heavenly Father.

2. Thank Him for our blessings.

3. Ask for the things we need.

4. Then close in the name of Jesus Christ.

Too often we miss #2 in the order of prayer—thank Him for our blessings. If we can remember we are daughters of God and He loves us . . . If we can remember He is aware of our thoughts and actions and the very desires of our hearts . . . If we can remember that He wants us to succeed and has promised to help us . . . If we can remember He always keeps His promises . . . we would realize we always have much to be grateful for. We would know our happiness doesn't depend on what has happened to us in the past, what our current circumstances are, or how other people respond to us. And we would never forget, no, we would never miss a single day expressing our love to Him. We wouldn't ask Him for anything until we had sufficiently thanked Him for our many blessings. Every morning and every night we would kneel in prayer. And silently all day we would carry a prayer in our hearts.

My friend Marcie Mower shared the following example of the importance of everyday prayer.

My son Jordan had his driver's license for about a week, when he lost his wallet. He came to me absolutely frantic for help. We discussed the procedure for what you do when you lose something, started retracing his footsteps, and talked about what to do in the future to prevent losing the item again. He was quick to dismiss some of the "steps," saying,

41

"No, it can't be there" and "I know I had it when I got home that night. So it HAS to be in the basement somewhere!"

As we retraced his footsteps one more time, he mentioned he went to the grocery store to buy a drink. I told him his wallet could be there, since he would have had to use it to pay for the drink. He said, "No," he didn't use his wallet. It was not at the grocery store. This went on for a day, with frustrations mounting for both of us as the wallet remained missing.

Finally, I told him to get on his knees and ask Heavenly Father where his wallet was. Twenty minutes later, he came upstairs with a smile on his face, and said he found it. He had prayed and received the answer immediately of where to find his wallet. It was at the grocery store. He called the store to verify, and it was indeed there.

Thirty minutes later, he returned with his wallet. I asked Jordan if he knew what to do next. He looked at me and said, "Always put my wallet and car keys in the same place every time I come in the house?" I said that would be helpful, but that was not what I was thinking about. I told him he needed to go downstairs, get back on his knees, and thank Heavenly Father for answering his prayer.

I then bore testimony to him that the most important prayer to Heavenly Father that day was the prayer from a desperate eighteen-year-old boy who was trying to find his missing wallet.

When my husband and I were called out of our stake to serve in leadership positions in a retirement/rehabilitation branch, one of our branch members shared with me her prayer of thanks. With permission, I include it here.

A Prayer of Thanksgiving
By Ruth C. Myers

I thank Thee, oh Father, for the freedoms that are mine—my country, my right to worship Thee as I see fit, and the free agency I enjoy.

I thank Thee for the people in my life, whom I love and who love me, for the friends and acquaintances who have filtered through my life like sunlight. Though their presence may be afar off, their warmth remains always with me.

I thank Thee for the great and small opportunities with which I am blessed—to learn skills, to discern truth, and to serve my fellow beings.

I thank Thee for the daily blessings which are bestowed upon me. I know my unworthiness, but Thou seest my potential. I thank Thee for blessing me in my efforts to be obedient, even when I fall short of my goals.

Thank Thee, Father, for listening to my prayers and for inspiring me to find solutions to my problems.

I thank Thee, too, for allowing me to have adversity in this earthly life that I might gain knowledge, develop compassion, empathy, and charity, and grow in spiritual strength.

I thank Thee most, Father, for the gospel of Jesus Christ, His great atoning sacrifice, and the opportunity to return to Thee.

I thank Thee for life.

Some days, in our haste, we need cues to remind us to pray and give thanks. Before certain health issues made it inadvisable to run, I was an avid runner. I ran every morning (except Sunday) before dawn. It was my habit to get up before the rest of the family, get myself organized for the day's activities, then head for my running shoes. I had a heavy rock engraved with the word "Pray." I put this rock in one of my shoes to remind me to pray before leaving the house. I experienced many instances of direct revelation due to those early-morning prayers, which always included a plea for my safety.

On one occasion, during my prayer I had the distinct impression it was not safe to go out that morning. I was disappointed, but took off my running shoes and chose another form of exercise for the day. I don't know what might have happened if I had gone, but with that kind of warning, I was not going to question it.

After my prayer on another day, I left the house in the dark and had run about a quarter of a mile when my toe caught the edge of a thick, metal plate left on the road due to construction. I found myself curling in a ball and rolling over the plate in a way I had never been taught. I stood up and looked back, realizing how easy it would have been for me to have broken a bone or received a concussion. Yet I had no bruises or breaks of any kind. I had performed the perfect tumbling roll! I was grateful for my prayer rock, and I had absolutely no doubt my prayer of safety had been heard.

We can set ourselves up to remember what we need to do. What cues we select will fit our habits. Maybe it's a note in the bathroom. Maybe it's a picture of Christ taped to the refrigerator. Anything will work that enables the thought process of remembering to pray.

There are times we do things for members of our family or our friends when they don't ask for them. Some things we do just because we love them and want to convey that love, or we can see they need help. For the same reasons, when we are obedient, God loves to do things for us also. Sometimes He expresses His love, not necessarily in answer to a specific request, but to give comfort or confirm He is personally aware of us.

A friend of mine, Mark Scoville, told me about just such an experience that happened to his great-grandfather, James E. Fisher. He related the story as follows:

> In the late 1800s, it was common to ask young married men to leave home and family to serve for two to five years. In 1891, at the age of 26, James was called on a mission to New Zealand for three and a half years. He and Elizabeth Stewart were married December 17, 1884, and had three children born to them between 1888 and 1891. When James was set apart as a missionary in 1892, he was told, "The Lord will provide food, raiment, and shelter for you."
>
> In New Zealand, Elder Fisher and his companion wondered and worried about their loved ones back home. One day as the missionaries rode along on their horses, they talked about how much they missed the good homemade bread so common back in Utah. Money from home had not yet arrived and they were hungry. Elder Fisher's companion suggested that they were alone and could dismount. They went into the woods and prayed. They expressed their desire to serve, as well as their love and concern for those back home.
>
> The two elders felt better, got back on their horses, and continued on their way. As they rode along, they noticed something just off the road. They dismounted and to their amazement found, wrapped in a white cloth, a fresh loaf of bread, which was the same kind of homemade bread they had talked about in their prayer. They rejoiced as they ate it, although it wasn't the bread that was so important, but the reassurance that Heavenly Father knew who and where they were.
>
> At that time, it took six weeks for a letter to get from Utah to New Zealand, and it cost 50 cents for postage, which

was then an enormous amount of money. Therefore, letters were sent only about once a month.

About three months after the elders found the bread on the trail, Elder Fisher's companion received a letter from his wife. She wrote that on the same day they made their discovery of the curious loaf of bread, she had been baking bread. When she opened her oven to remove it, one of the pans was empty and a white cloth that had been on the table was gone. She had been home all the time and saw no one come or go.

The two missionaries had received an answer to prayer. The loaf of bread came to symbolize for them that Heavenly Father, who had sent them to New Zealand, was supporting them and watching over their families.

I have personally experienced miracles of such magnitude, but more often the answers to prayer and the show of love from my Father come in subtle ways and play out over time.

I suppose one of the reasons I feel so strongly about this subject is because of an experience in my own life that left me with an absolute witness and appreciation for the great power of prayer and the priesthood. I share this personal experience in the hope that it will affect your faith and testimony as it did mine.

As a young mother, I had a dream. At the time I thought it was an odd dream, nothing likely to ever come to pass. I saw myself at my parents' home in Arizona. I was sick and lying on the couch. My mother stood at the foot of the couch. My father was in a recliner chair adjacent to me. I had young children with me, one a toddler in diapers, and they were walking around near the couch. I thought the dream odd and unlikely to come to pass because I didn't travel with my children without my husband. So I completely forgot about it.

Several years later, while living in Colorado, I found myself alone with my children. My husband was in Texas, getting training from the company he worked for. He was going to be gone for several weeks. About two weeks into his absence, I had the distinct prompting I needed to go home, that is to my parents' home in Arizona. I didn't know why. I just couldn't deny the feelings. I thought about my grandparents (who lived in the same town as my parents), especially my grandfather, and wondered if something was going to happen to him and I needed to see him to say good-bye. I really couldn't think of any other reason for me to go home.

I couldn't shake the feeling, so after a few days, I called my parents and told them how I felt. I wouldn't take the risk to drive with my children (I had three at the time), so I asked my father if he would come and get us. Dad was a schoolteacher. He said if I could wait until the weekend, he and my mother would make the trip.

They left on a Friday, right after school, drove to Colorado, picked up the children and me, and drove back to Arizona. I'm not even sure he took three days. It might have only been two. He didn't miss any work, and I made it there safely with my children.

I visited my grandparents. They seemed to be doing fine. I filled my time by playing with my children, taking them to the park, and enjoying time at home with my parents. After about two or three days, though, I started to feel sick. I thought it was the flu. Not a simple flu; I couldn't hold anything down either direction for several days. I couldn't take care of my children. I couldn't do anything, and we finally decided I'd better see a doctor.

My parents didn't go to doctors much in those days. And my being from out of town didn't help. We made some phone calls, but couldn't find a doctor who would see me. At last we located a doctor who had just graduated from medical school, had not set up a practice yet, but would be willing to see me in a friend's office. My sister drove me to the doctor's office, where I was diagnosed with food poisoning and sent home with directions to drink lots of fluids. That was pretty ridiculous since by this time I could hardly swallow.

Remember that dream? Well, *I was at my parents' home in Arizona. I was sick and lying on the couch. My mother stood at the foot of the couch. My father was in a recliner chair adjacent to me. I had young children with me, one a toddler in diapers, and they were walking around near the couch.* My mother said to my father, "She's as white as a sheet. I think we're going to lose her. I'm going to call the doctor."

I heard Mother talking to the doctor about taking me to the hospital, and I said to her, "I'm not going to the hospital unless he will meet me at the front door with a wheelchair. I can't walk." The doctor agreed and my parents took me to the hospital.

After an examination, the doctor said he couldn't figure out what was wrong and he called in a specialist, a surgeon. The specialist ran tests and did X-rays for a couple days. I hurt everywhere. The pain was so intense, the highest doses of pain medication hardly made a difference. Even opening my eyes became a struggle.

My husband arrived from Texas and the doctor called a meeting in my room. Lining the walls were doctors and nurses. I didn't know why my case deserved that much attention. The doctor explained he could not determine the cause of my trouble and recommended exploratory surgery. He said, "I don't know if she can withstand the surgery. At this point, it's our only hope. If it is her appendix, you need to know she will never have more children. When the appendix ruptures, the poison fills the female organs first. We need to get her into surgery as soon as possible."

I said, "I'm not going into surgery until I have a priesthood blessing." Although he was not a member of The Church of Jesus Christ of Latter-day Saints and had no understanding of the power of the priesthood, he honored my wishes and said he would wait, but we needed to hurry. So my dad came from the school and he and my husband gave me a blessing. Just prior to the blessing I told them, "I need you to bless me that I'll be able to have more children. There are more children that belong in my family." The blessing was pronounced with the authority and power of the priesthood.

The next thing I remember was waking up in intensive care connected to many tubes and pumps, and sitting at the side of my bed was the surgeon. He seemed to be in a daze. He was shaking his head back and forth, back and forth, and saying, "I don't understand. I don't understand."

I interrupted him and said, "What don't you understand?"

He responded, "I don't understand how you could possibly be alive! Every organ in your body was filled with peritonitis, every organ except your female organs."

And I said, "Would you like me to tell you about the priesthood?"

My parents and family offered many prayers in my behalf. The next several weeks were rough, but I made it. And later when I was discharged from his care, I asked the doctor why people were making such a fuss over my case. I said, "With medicine as it is today, you save everyone with a ruptured appendix, don't you?"

He said, "You just don't understand. We can save just about everyone if we catch it before the appendix ruptures. We can save most if we catch it shortly after the appendix ruptures. But I've looked through the medical records and I can find no record of anyone ever living through what you've just experienced. Your appendix ruptured at least five to seven days before you came to the hospital. If you had remained in your home in Colorado, your children would have found you dead!"

It took six months for me to be strong enough to lift more than a fork. But over the years, I doubled the size of my family. This much I know: God is in charge. He is a loving Heavenly Father. Plans were made in advance to spare my life. Without a doubt I know it was the Spirit that compelled me to go to my parents' home. And there is no question in my mind that prayers are answered and the great healing power of the priesthood is real.

The second thread of power and safety is doing our part to communicate with our Father through prayer. And the secret to unlocking that power is leaning on the Lord with complete trust.

NOTES:

1. Susanna McMahon, *The Portable Therapist* (New York: Dell Publishing, 1992), 221.

2. Elder Parley P. Pratt, *Key to the Science of Theology*, 9th ed. (Salt Lake City: Deseret Book, 1965), 101.

3. Elder LeGrand Richards, in Conference Report, Apr. 1966, 112; or *Improvement Era*, June 1966, 540.

4. President Abraham Lincoln, in William J. Federer, *America's God and Country Encyclopedia of Quotations* (FAME Publishing, Inc., 1996), 377.

CHAPTER 4

The Word of God

—✦—

Be of good cheer, and do not fear, for I the Lord am with you, and will stand by you.
— D&C 68:6

—✦—

Three verbs might describe the message of the previous chapter—pray, listen, and act. Another that was mentioned was lean—lean on the Lord. What does that mean, to lean on the Lord? It means we look with confidence to Him for answers and solutions. It means we accept His will for us. It means we trust He will keep His promises to help us. It means we praise and thank Him for the guidance and peace He sends and for His unconditional love and example.

Stephanie L. Yates, a mother of four, told me about one of her learning experiences regarding leaning on the Lord. Here, in her own words, is her story.

> We were building a new home. Our previous home sold before it was even on the market. However, the buyers, a

51

young couple right out of college, demanded several repairs. These repairs were minor things that my husband could fix himself, except for a part of the roof that needed mending. We knew it needed to be fixed because we previously had several minor leaks. To save $500, he decided to repair it himself. Not knowing the first thing about roofs, he bought all the materials, and on the hottest day of the summer, went up on the roof and put on a new layer of undercoating and shingles.

We were in a rental home now, waiting for our new home to be finished. We had exactly $1,500 after closing costs for all the new stuff we needed for the house. Fifteen hundred dollars might seem like a lot. However, when you start thinking about curtains, curtain rods, rugs, storm doors, blinds, and so on, it would have to be stretched.

We were in this rental home two months and our new home would be completed in another month. These months had been extremely rainy. One Friday night when my husband was ready to leave for an overnighter with the scouts, a large envelope arrived in the mail. Inside it were horrible pictures of a bedroom in our previous home where rain had pooled on the roof, causing the ceiling to cave in, ruining a wall and the carpet. The buyers had their inspector back out and he said it was probably our fault, as it appeared the roof had not been properly fixed. They were asking for $1500 for the costs of all the repairs. If we didn't pay, they said they might take us to court to sue for the damages. My heart sunk. Fifteen hundred dollars—that was exactly what we had for our new home. I asked Dwight what we should do. He said, "You pray about it and decide." With that, he was out the door to camp with the scouts!

I prayed fervently to Heavenly Father, "What should we do?"

His immediate answer: "What would you expect if you were them?"

"But Father," I said, "what should we do?"

"Put yourself in their shoes."

"But, should we pay them the money?"

Again: "What would you expect if you were them?"

I knew right then and there I needed to call them and tell them I would have a check for $1,500 in the mail the next day. I picked up the phone and spoke with the wife, apologizing about what they had been through. I told her I would write a check and it would be in the mail the next day. She broke down in tears, thanking me many times, saying after buying the house they only had $1,500 left and if we would not pay for the damages, all of their money would have to go to the repairs. She continued saying they would not be able to buy all the new things she wanted for the house if they had to pay for the damages. Among other things, she mentioned new curtains, rugs, blinds, and so on. Crying, she thanked me, said they probably would not have sued us because it couldn't be proven since it had rained several times since they moved in, and she hung up. By that time I was crying, knowing that I would not have the money for my new things.

I feel you need to know that by this time we had been married for 28 years. We had just had three of our four children return from missions and graduate from college (plus college graduates of a daughter-in-law and a son-in-law). (We said when our children married, we didn't gain a son/daughter-in-law; we inherited another college student!) Our previous home had "pre-four-teenager/college-student/missionary" décor. Our towels were rags. Every kitchen appliance was harvest gold, and even though I worked for the telephone company, we still had an old, harvest gold rotary dial phone. I was ready for some new things!

Again, I got on my knees and prayed to my Father, thanking him for directing me to do the right thing. I was immediately overwhelmed with a feeling that it all would work out, and that I would be called to be the stake Relief Society president!

My husband arrived home late Saturday afternoon and asked me what I decided and what I did about it. I told him what happened and he remarked that he knew that's what I would decide. He just wanted me to decide that! He admitted he probably didn't fix the roof properly and was just trying to save a buck.

The next day, Sunday, the stake president called me into his office and called me to be the stake Relief Society president. I told him I had been praying Friday night (I did not go into the entire story) and the Holy Ghost confirmed to me that he would call me to this position. He said that the previous week he had three sisters whom he was praying about for that calling, and it wasn't until Friday night that he knew it should be me.

That same Sunday afternoon we received a call from our builder. He said we weren't going to believe it, and he had never made that mistake before, but he was going over the papers for the closing and he had overcharged us for several things. He said he double billed us for part of the deck and forgot to reduce the cost when we changed from rock to brick on the front of our house. He said when we closed in three weeks, we would need exactly $1,500 less than he had previously told us.

Call it prayer, paying tithing, whatever you may. It was a testimony to me that we are individually watched over and cared for by a loving Heavenly Father.

One scripture comes clearly to mind in regards to Stephanie's story. Coincidentally it's one mentioned in the last chapter by Naomi Randall—"Trust in the Lord with all thine heart; and lean not unto thine own understanding" (Proverbs 3:5).

Elisha, in the Old Testament, also dramatically experienced being directed and cared for by the Lord. The king of Syria sent his horses and chariots to destroy Elisha. But Elisha's power was great because, like Stephanie, he trusted in the Lord. When Elisha's servant asked him how they were going to handle the situation, Elisha said, "Fear not: for they that be with us are more than they that be with them" (2 Kings 6:16). Then Elisha asked for the servant to be able to see the hosts waiting to help them. The Lord opened the servant's eyes and he saw the horses and chariots of fire around Elisha. When keeping our covenants, we can be assured the Lord will help us in our struggles just as he did Elisha.

When I was an anxious, single parent, I went to my bishop for a priesthood blessing. I was impressed by that blessing and I'd like to share a few points he made. To my recollection he said, "Put your anxiety at rest. Be peaceful, very peaceful . . . Those on the other side are behind you and in front of you and on every side to help you. Know you are not alone. Those in this stake and ward are your friends and will help you. Cease to worry. . . Satan will try to influence you in the same way as the Savior. Take it to the Lord. Listen with the Spirit instead of with your head. There are such wonderful blessings in store for you. You will be tried. You must be sure of yourself before the blessings can come."

Notice the following three critical elements presented in the blessing:

- You are not alone.

• Satan will try to influence you.

• Take it to the Lord and listen with your heart.

The experience Stephanie shared, Elisha's story, and the blessing I received clearly solves the question, "How do we overcome our enemies, both the seen and the unseen?" The answer—through mighty prayer and leaning on the Lord.

We cannot afford to be careless and allow Satan to confuse us with deception and counterfeit doctrine. In addition to prayer, the Apostle Paul said to "put on the whole armour of God, that ye may be able to stand against the wiles of the devil" (Ephesians 6:11).

The armor of God Paul referred to includes acting with faith and complete integrity and clinging to the word of God, or, in other words, knowing and keeping God's commandments. Later, in the Americas, Nephi gave the same advice when he explained what the rod of iron was that leads to the tree of life: "It was the word of God; and whoso would hearken unto the word of God, and would hold fast unto it, they would never perish; neither could the temptations and the fiery darts of the adversary overpower them unto blindness, to lead them away to destruction" (1 Nephi 15:24).

The only way we can hold fast to the word of God is to study it. The word of God is the Bible, the Book of Mormon, the Doctrine and Covenants, the Pearl of Great Price, and the words of the living prophets provided in official Church magazines. For ourselves, we can also regard our patriarchal blessings as the word of God. They are inspired, personal revelations from God specifically for each of us—our own personal scripture. Learning true doctrine allows us to unmask deception and recognize the false. Then we can be braced for even the very hardest lessons of life.

56

Kamilla Fisker, a young law student from Denmark, told me why reading the word of God—the scriptures—was important to her. She said, "My branch president gave us a promise—if we would read the scriptures just ten minutes a day, we would stay spiritually strong. I wanted to see if it was true. So I tried, and it is true. I've felt a difference. And staying strong in the Church is important, because there are so many temptations. Satan wears a disguise and it can be very difficult to see through him."

The importance of the scriptures is clear. Lehi knew his family needed the records for guidance. He felt so strongly about it, he risked his sons' lives by sending Nephi and his brothers back to Jerusalem to get the records. How can the scriptures help us if they only sit on the shelf and collect dust? When we choose not to read the scriptures every day, a subtle change occurs. Our focus shifts away from making every effort to become a daughter of God. We must never treat these precious protective tools lightly.

Before reading, we can ask Heavenly Father to help us understand and retain what we read. Just as important, we can specifically ask Him to help us see how the scriptures pertain to us, how we can apply what we read in our daily lives.

Stephanie Yates (quoted earlier) gave me a good example of an object lesson she attempted to use when teaching her favorite scripture to seminary students:

> *The glory of God is intelligence, or, in other words, light and truth. Light and truth forsake that evil one (D&C 93:36–37).*

I was teaching early morning seminary and we were studying Church history in section 93 of the D&C. The teacher's manual suggested giving the students a verse or two beginning about verse 19 and continuing through verse 39, and have them identify what truth there was in their assigned verses. The young lady that was assigned verses 36 and 37 said this: "Light and truth will always forsake evil. Think of it as a dark room without windows. A light is on in the hall and you open the door to the room. Dark does not enter the hall. Light enters the room."

I had previously used an object lesson and tried to get the room completely dark by covering the windows to the seminary room, which was the family room in our home. I was to light a small candle, then a larger one, then turn on a flashlight, then turn on the lights to the room to signify what can happen when you allow the light of Christ to enter by praying, fasting, reading your scriptures—you know, all the standard answers. No matter what I did, I could not get the room completely dark, even though it was only 6:00 in the morning!

We had a wonderful discussion about these verses, also discussing the object lesson. I told them no matter how hard I tried that previous week, I couldn't get the room as dark as I wanted it. We likened that to all of Heavenly Father's children. They are the same way. They all have a bit of light, and it is up to us to open our proverbial spiritual doors to them and let the light in.

The saying "Work your schedule around what is truly important rather than try to work what is important into your schedule" has real meaning when we think about committing to never miss a day of reading the scriptures. As Kamilla Fisker reminded us, just ten minutes a day can make a difference.

I remember when I first made that commitment to myself. I wrote it in my personal goals. It was written like this: "I read my scriptures each evening before I go to bed." After that, I never missed a day, no matter how tired I was or how early I would have to start the next day. Obviously, I was more alert some evenings than others to what I was reading. Sometimes I only read one verse to keep my commitment to the Lord and to myself. I remember thinking, *"Maybe it will work for me like it does at times for others. Maybe if I just randomly open the book and read a verse, it will be handpicked for me by the Lord."* I'd open the book, close my eyes, point with my finger to a verse, and read it. And sure enough that one single verse answered a question, confirmed a thought, or pointed me in a direction that was significant to me at that time in my life.

One of those verses was so vital for me I later printed it on poster paper and attached it to the refrigerator door so I'd see it often. It's the verse I mentioned in the previous chapter as my favorite—"For God hath not given us the spirit of fear; but of power, and of love, and of a sound mind" (2 Timothy 1:7).

Since goals make a difference more often if they are specific, I rewrote my goal like this: "I read at least one verse from the scriptures each evening before I go to bed." Often I'd read one verse and it would cause me to look something up, and by the time I finished reading, I'd read a chapter or two. Those sessions of searching and pondering increased my love and appreciation for the scriptures. I grew in gospel understanding, and I was taught the Lord's definition of personal accountability.

One year I chose to use colored pencils to mark my scriptures. I used blue to mark verses that referenced the Holy Ghost, orange for faith, green for women, and red for verses I found particularly important to me. At the end of a year of reading, I realized verses about the Holy Ghost were linked with the words "power" and "Christ." That made me think all the more about how important it is to listen for the promptings from the Holy Ghost. And because of my consistent reading, I felt influenced to be more forgiving. I felt more sure of myself, safer, and more spiritually and physically prepared to meet my challenges.

Of course there's nothing special about reading the scriptures in the evening, except to me. That is the best time for me.

Morning, noon, or night—it really doesn't matter, except for what works consistently for the individual.

Physical exercise enhances our good feelings about ourselves. It can help alleviate pain and cause us to be more alert. Not that it should replace physical exercise, but it's good to know that the exercise of reading the scriptures every day also enhances our good feelings about ourselves. And having the scriptures on our minds daily also helps alleviate our emotional pain and causes us to be more alert. It is much more difficult to feel terrible about ourselves when we are learning about God and His ways. It becomes much more difficult to focus on negative feelings when we are asking for guidance from the Lord and acting on that guidance. By faithfully reading the scriptures, we become empowered with clear direction and the companionship of the Spirit. And as Helaman told his sons, *we cannot fail* (see Helaman 5:12). The Lord has the answers for us if we take the necessary steps to receive them.

By seeking knowledge through study and prayer, women of today are strengthened to face the adversary, just as the early pioneer women did. We overcome the forces of evil by developing a strong testimony of truth, identifying our personal relationship with the Father, drawing strength from Him, and relying on Him.

The third thread of power and safety is to put on the full armor of God by acting with faith and clinging to the scriptures—the word of God.

CHAPTER 5

Awareness

Wherefore, beware lest ye are deceived; and that ye may not be deceived seek ye earnestly the best gifts, always remembering for what they are given.
—D&C 46:8

There's a profound, three-fold power that comes with regular reading of the scriptures: We gain knowledge, we gain the companionship of the Spirit, and we feel more confident in making good choices and in the outcome of those choices.

We gain knowledge. We can never know too much. Depending on our circumstances, we can read the same verses one day that teach us something different the next. Not really "different" because the scriptures don't change. But they enlighten us differently, depending on the answers we're seeking and the experiences we're having.

With the companionship of the Spirit, we gain awareness when we consistently read the scriptures. That awareness enables us to have faith in our own judgment. When we come up against difficult situations, we're reminded of stories we've read that will help us be aware not only of our surroundings but also of actions we should take. The stories in the scriptures are written for us, and they give us blueprints to follow for our safety.

When we are grounded with the knowledge that comes from the scriptures, we feel closer to our Father, and our confidence in Him providing needed direction gains more solid footing.

Like Stephanie (mentioned in the previous chapter), Darlene Forbes (not her real name) studied the scriptures and learned to lean on the Lord. Darlene's story is dramatic and far too common, but her ability to recognize her mistakes and take appropriate steps for her protection is exemplary.

> Looking back, I can see the red flags waving frantically. They tried to get my attention, warning me about my courtship with Russell. However, while I was in the thick of it, they were difficult to see. It had been three years since narrowly escaping an abusive marriage to Deen. After years of counseling, I thought I was ready to try dating again and felt confident I would never allow myself to be deceived like that again.

> I met a charming man, who, although he had a string of "bad luck" (red flag!), seemed decent, kind, and caring. The confusion I felt while in my marriage to Deen returned again with Russell (red flag!), and it felt alarmingly familiar. It started seeping in gradually, getting louder and louder with each passing week, until finally I had to take it out and look at it. As soon as I did, I became aware of two things: either I was (1) still very broken from my marriage to Deen and was confusing Deen and Russell, or (2) I was involved with another abusive man and history was repeating itself.

> I grabbed my journal and made two columns. In the first column I wrote how Deen and Russell were alike. My plan

was to write in the second column the ways they were different. As I worked on my lists, it was as if the veil parted and I had a clarity that can only come when we are still and the Holy Ghost descends upon us. Being still like that takes patience, especially when emotions are running high. As I worked on my lists and being still, allowing the Spirit to reveal to me the differences and similarities between the two men, I realized I didn't have anything in the second column (red flag!). This still didn't tell me whether I was broken and confused or was making the same mistake. However, I quickly realized it didn't matter. I was in no shape to make any kind of commitment until I had this figured out.

Russell panicked when I started backing out. The relationship fell apart, and I broke off the engagement. He quickly turned vicious and mean and the threats to "bring me down" and "make me pay" started coming (red flag!). I had my answer. I was repeating a past mistake.

Over the course of several months, Russell would not leave me alone. He called, emailed, texted me constantly, sent me flowers, even after I begged him to leave me alone. At first he appeared to be a man with a broken heart, who simply could not let go. Then his constant, unwanted attentions escalated and I started getting angry. I got so angry that I finally called the police and was put in touch with a domestic violence advocate. When I gave her Russell's name, I could hear her talking to the detective next to her saying, "Russell's next victim has finally surfaced."

The domestic violence advocate carefully explained to me that I was being stalked. Russell was a dangerous man and had tried to kill two of his wives. He was a career criminal who made his living stealing and conning his way through women's bank accounts and hearts, and my safety was truly at risk. I asked for protection for me and my children, since we all knew I was his next victim. We just didn't know when he would strike. Sadly, they told me they could offer me no protection until he harmed me or my children.

After I hung up the phone and the shock of my situation wore off, I knelt beside my bedside and offered a fervent prayer for protection for me and my children. In this prayer I recognized the arm of flesh could not save me, and my only hope was to rely on the arm of the Lord for protection. Although Russell continued to give me problems for the next few years, I continued to rely on the arm of the Lord for protection, followed the promptings I received, and remained unharmed.

Again, how do we overcome our enemies, both the seen and the unseen? We listen with the Spirit instead of with our heads, like the bishop told me in the priesthood blessing; we lean on the Lord.

In addition to having knowledge and an individual testimony, women today must be observant and consciously increase their personal power of awareness. One of the best defenses against evil is awareness. When striving to be aware of our surroundings, we are more able to recognize the subtle temptations of Satan and his followers.

Some time ago, I visited a ward in another state. The Sunday School teacher told us about moving to an apartment neighboring a busy street and under a flight line for a major airline. At first the noise was really overwhelming. They were so disturbed, he and his family could hardly sleep or go about their daily activities in the house. Then as the days, weeks, and months came and went, they became accustomed to the noise and clamor, and it no longer wrinkled their pattern of living. In fact, they reached a point where they didn't even hear the noise anymore. In that case, it was a blessing they just got used to it. But in many cases, it is essential we consciously observe and be aware of our environment. If something appears out of the ordinary in a negative way or seems inappropriate, most often it is.

Because of the gift of agency, we choose what we do and what we do not do. We choose which thoughts and feelings to act upon and which to ignore. Paying attention to our feelings (even if we can't logically explain them) and our observations can increase our level of safety. Take for example my experience with early-morning prayer and deciding not to go running (mentioned in a previous chapter). That was clearly a warning for my safety. I don't know what would have happened if I had not paid attention to that prompting, but gratefully I don't have to worry about that now.

We may receive a prompting of warning along with a disturbing observation. Here is an example. We moved to a new neighborhood in northern Illinois. It was a beautiful rural setting. Picture the grass being green, flowers opening their springtime buds, and birds happily chirping in the trees. In learning that my next-door neighbors were members of the Church, I knocked on their door to meet them. The husband answered the knock in his bathrobe, saying his wife was not home. He was all smiles, appeared to visit freely, even walked outside, following me along the sidewalk near his home.

From the moment he opened the door, I felt something wasn't right and felt prompted to leave. It seemed odd that he was so comfortable in his bathrobe having a conversation with me. I know this will sound strange, but it seemed as though everything turned gray—the grass was not so green, the flowers lacked color, and the birds were mute. I kept the conversation short and left quickly. I had that uncomfortable feeling every time I was around him, even with interactions at church. I don't know how long it was, maybe a year later, when I learned he had been unfaithful to his wife multiple times and she was suing him for divorce. My experience is an example of observation coupled with a warning prompting.

The act of consciously observing our environment and noticing things out of the ordinary can save our lives. When I was a schoolteacher, it was my habit to rise early and run at the school track before going to work. Usually a few other individuals ran at the same time. But one morning, I was on the track alone when I noticed a man approaching. The sun had not come up, yet this man was wearing sunglasses. I thought about that observation for only a moment before taking my pepper spray out of my pouch, extending my arm in an exaggerated fashion so the man would see, and obviously cocking the spray. The man directly turned around and left the track. I believe being observant saved me from harm that morning.

Bad things happen to good people. Remember, safety ranks as a primary need for all people. The longing for safety is more basic than for sleep or food or sex. We must remain aware of our surroundings and not allow ourselves to stay in an unsafe environment if there is any means of escape. We must not ignore or allow any kind of abusive behavior, overlook our observations that signal warnings for our safety, or disregard a warning prompting. In order to stay aware, we have to open our senses and interpret the signs and signals our heart, eyes, and brain receive.

Asking Heavenly Father to help us be alert and see things as they really are will enable us to see what we can do to be safe. Aside from that, what are some of the things we can look for to increase our level of safety?

- Beware of inconsistent patterns of behavior, behavior that intimidates or degrades another, or behavior that harms or exerts control over others. Be observant of the little things that add up, like words the other person uses to

manipulate how we feel about him or her or the situation—
"Why, you know I wouldn't have done anything like that
if you hadn't . . ." Step back and watch for how the other
individual tells a truthful-sounding but still untruthful
story.

- Beware of the tendency to want things to be good so
badly that we deny reality. When it is present, trust
that uncomfortable feeling. Fear must not be allowed
to immobilize us. Have the courage to make the choice
of change when an environment takes us away from the
Spirit.

- Beware of the stranger who approaches when help is not
requested. Although the person may turn out to be just
a kindly stranger, watch for other signals. If rebuffed,
does he or she offer a slight insult just to get engaged in
conversation? Or does he or she offer counterfeit charity—
"Let me help you with that heavy grocery bag"—only to
turn around and exploit the shopper's sense of obligation?
If an offer is unsolicited, refuse with a definite "no." If
the stranger ignores the "no" and insists on helping, never
negotiate. Loudly repeat by saying, "I said no," without
an explanation. In most cases, the stranger who refuses
to hear the "no" is trying to control the situation to
accomplish a sinister purpose. Bring the context of any
meeting with a stranger into conscious thought.

- Beware of anyone—not just strangers—who shows no
respect for privacy, asks out-of-place personal questions,
pays undue attention to us, and when in our homes
with us alone (such as a repairman), wants to know
if others are home or if and when we expect others to
arrive home.

- Beware of unhealthy distraction. Fear can be an unhealthy distraction, if we remain focused on the fear and fail to hear what is actually being said or done. Watch for unjustified familiarity, unlikely warmth, or unnecessary details in conversation (especially with a stranger) that might distract from what the other person is actually doing. Watch for body language that does not match verbal expressions. Even a person's voice tone can reveal his or her real intent. If the tone is hostile and the words pleasant, respond to the tone. We can ask ourselves, is he or she charming, or is he or she trying to charm me? There's a definite difference.

- Beware of the other person always being on the defense—always excusing himself or herself from any wrongdoing. Especially watch the other person's attitude. Does he or she act with an undue sense of entitlement? Be quiet and observe. Are reasonable answers given for reasonable questions? Or does the other person attempt to play mind games by twisting the truth or diverting the conversation away from answering the questions?

- Beware of anyone who tries to shift our focus away from making and keeping covenants, anyone who attempts to belittle living prophets, or anyone who professes Christ while spewing subtle anti-Christ statements.

- Beware of manipulative behavior that takes advantage of our weaknesses and tries to inspire us with the idea that we are no good, always wrong, prone to make mistakes, or completely dependent on the other person. Force the brain to stay in gear so you can evaluate information truthfully. Remembering who we are—daughters of God—and leaning on Him for discernment, coupled with our thoughtful observations, will make it possible for us to sense something is amiss and act appropriately for our benefit and safety.

- Never use headphones or other devices that disable hearing while running, walking, hiking, or otherwise exercising alone outside. Our hearing is a very important survival sense. Sight is another. When that uncomfortable feeling is present, look squarely at strangers and look squarely at the environment. Doing so not only conveys to the other person we are not easy prey, but it also provides us with knowledge of our surroundings in case an escape becomes necessary.

If we pay attention to our surroundings and listen to the promptings of the Spirit, we can know when we are in the presence of danger and be guided through risky situations. Here are a few things we can do when we sense our safety might be compromised:

- Ahead of time, choose a code word to use with family, friends, and neighbors when assistance is needed.

- Ahead of time, think of a safe house to retreat to—a friend, family, coworker, shelter.

- Ahead of time, call a domestic violence hotline or local shelter to learn about the laws and other resources. To find out about the domestic violence services in your community, contact the National Domestic Violence Hotline—800-799-SAFE (800-799-7233)—or www .ndvh.org.

- Ahead of time, instruct children about keeping themselves safe by hiding or going to a neighbor's house and not protecting us.

- If an individual we live with behaves in such a way that we feel our safety is truly at risk, talk about it with someone we trust. If there is violence, do not keep it a secret, and get out. Never allow abuse to override our natural instinct to be safe.

- In a dangerous situation, focus on our environment to determine possible escape routes.

Of most importance, trust our judgment and our feelings. No one knows better than we do how dangerous the situation is. The Spirit can detect and warn us about the slightest variance from truth. If we're not sure what it sounds like or feels like to have the Spirit speak to us, we can ask Heavenly Father to teach us. And over time, our sensitivity to the still small voice will increase and we will recognize the warnings and direction available from the ultimate protector and judge between good and evil—the Holy Ghost. When we do our part to have the Spirit with us and we trust the Spirit, we cannot fail.

Awareness is a choice. Consciously choosing or not choosing—either way we make a choice. A person's agency is his or her supreme power here on earth. No other creature has this power to the extent we do. We are constantly exercising it, whether for our benefit or not. We are not accountable for the abusive actions of others. However, as we realize and accept our responsibility for the choices we make and the consequences we create, we can ensure a safer, more peaceful environment for ourselves and for our families. We do not need to always be on edge or suspicious of others, unless we find or feel reason. Living in today's world, however, is not a time to be passive. Always be aware.

We have to live with the consequences of our choices. It is a given that we will make mistakes. It's not possible to make perfect choices all the time. But like Darlene, it is possible to consistently make better choices that we can live with and grow from when we respect and trust ourselves, set reasonable limits, and have a clear understanding of our identity—daughters of God.

Our Heavenly Father does not want us to cower or wallow in misery. He expects us to square our shoulders, roll up our sleeves, and overcome our challenges. When we overcome our fears through preparation and awareness, we can face what comes with courage and move forward. Courage is not defined in the dictionary necessarily as a lack of fear. Rather, courage is defined as the quality of mind that enables a person to face difficulty, danger, or pain in spite of fear. Having the courage to assess our situation, no matter how frightening, to lean on the Lord, and to move forward is courageous. It is the way of the heroine.

The fourth thread of power and safety is increasing our personal power of awareness while clinging to the word of God and leaning on the Lord.

CHAPTER 6

Obedience

"If ye shall keep the commandments of . . . God, . . . ye shall prosper in the land, and your enemies shall have no power over you.
— Mosiah 2:31

As we study, ponder, and come to know the word of God, our confidence grows. By reading the accounts of those people who fought on the Lord's side, we gain insight and strength to fight our own battles and make wise choices. Knowing the word of God doesn't come all at once, however. As mentioned before, we can read a verse from the scriptures one day and find great meaning. Then another day we can read the same verse, while experiencing different circumstances in our lives, and learn something new or find a new application for the same scripture.

Learning to act with awareness is like reading the scriptures. We learn precept upon precept about what we should be looking for and how we should be interpreting what we see and feel. Knowledge of the truth of our surroundings enables us to make safe choices.

The sons of Mosiah were successful because they "waxed strong in knowledge of the truth;" they "searched the scriptures diligently, that they might know the word of God" (see Alma 17:2).

What does it mean to wax strong in knowledge? The verb "wax" means to increase in extent, quantity, intensity, or power. Think of melted wax falling one drop upon another, one layer building on the other until the thickness and strength allows it to stand by itself.

Our knowledge of the word of God and His ways, and our knowledge gained through awareness, builds as we put in the effort to learn over time and with experience. As that knowledge grows in extent, giving us increased power, we develop confidence in ourselves and assurance that God values us and wants us to be safe and successful.

We can take the wax analogy a little further. If a wick is placed in the center of that strong, built-up wax and is lit, it can bring light and hope to others. And that's what happened to the sons of Mosiah. They studied, prayed, and fasted, and then taught with great power and brought "many to the knowledge of the truth" (see Alma 17:4). In spite of their many dangerous and difficult experiences, they accomplished their missions.

The same is true for us; through preparation, we can wax strong in knowledge of the truth. The scriptures and our increased power of awareness can light our path, strengthen our resolve, and give us a firm anchor to hold on to. Remember, however, that we are responsible as we learn the word of God and see our surroundings more clearly; we must act upon that knowledge.

> For of him [her] unto whom much is given much is required; and he [she] who sins against the greater light shall receive the greater condemnation. Ye call upon my name for revelations, and I give them unto you; and inasmuch as ye

keep not my sayings, which I give unto you, ye become trans-gressors; and justice and judgment are the penalty which is affixed unto my law. (D&C 82:3–4)

Latter-day Saint women have more opportunity to wax strong in knowledge of the truth than any other group of women in the world. They have the gift of the Holy Ghost, inspired scripture, living prophets, access to priesthood power, and count-less opportunities for unique leadership training and experience. We have the opportunity to make covenants unlike any other women. The ordinances of baptism and confirmation alone offer incomparable rights to the companionship of the Spirit. Couple that with the temple endowment, and truly waxing strong in knowledge of the truth is certainly available to every one of us. This reservoir of knowledge and support can fuel our determi-nation to succeed and fulfill our individual missions. Does it come free? Of course not. We have to put in the effort to build up the wax, so to speak. That wick core can only stand tall and light the way when it is firmly embedded in sturdy wax.

And when we make covenants and choose not to keep them, we choose to allow Satan to have power over us. The old saying "use it or lose it" is really true in regards to main-taining a testimony, having continued companionship of the Spirit, and waxing strong in the knowledge of the truth. In every sense, we must be true to the word of God we've come to know, and we must act on the promptings we receive through our increased power of awareness. In the sweet, quiet times and when we face our own dangerous and difficult experiences, we must consistently "walk it like we talk it" to be spiritually guided and protected. We cannot escape the immense, personal accountability. Fulfilling our missions in life and our eternal safety depend on it.

When we are prepared and "walk it like we talk it," fear dis-solves. To "walk the talk," we exhibit internally and externally an unwavering light—a full commitment to being fair, acting with awareness and integrity, steadfast in living our values, and courageous in keeping our promises to God. Keeping those promises is how we gain the power to handle whatever we're asked to endure in life. It is not only the safest way, but the only way to eternal happiness.

Here are some of the basics:

- We humble ourselves and repent of our sins and forgive others for theirs.

- We keep the Sabbath Day holy, worshipping and reverencing God.

- We serve those who are in need.

- We follow the counsel of the Prophet to manage our finances appropriately and obtain the suggested food and emergency supplies.

- We care for our bodies by eating, sleeping, exercising, and dressing appropriately.

- We faithfully pay our tithing and attend our church meetings.

- We act in virtue.

- We accept callings and fulfill them to the best of our abilities.

- We magnify our womanhood by embracing motherhood with a happy countenance and/or nurturing others with a giving, happy heart.

- We make and keep sacred covenants and, where possible, attend the temple regularly.

To condense that list, here is a paraphrased version taken from Alma's sayings in the Book of Mormon (see Mosiah 18:8–10). When one of my grandchildren is baptized, I make a plaque for him or her with this saying:

You have been baptized in the name of the Lord,
making a promise to serve Him and keep His commandments.
As you help others with their work, and help those that are
sad or lonely,
and stand as a witness of God at all times and in all things
and in all places wherever you may be,
His spirit will direct your path in all you do.

In other words, we remember who we are and who we want to become, and we look and sincerely act the part. I don't mean "act" as in entertain. I mean "act" as in we do. And in the doing process, we are lifted up and able to bear all things, and we come to know it is by the Lord we are sustained.

In 1936, President Heber J. Grant made a direct statement that covers this issue well:

There is but one path of safety to the Latter-day Saints, and that is the path of duty. It is not testimony, it is not marvelous manifestations, it is not knowing that the Gospel of Jesus Christ is true, . . . it is not actually knowing that the Savior is the Redeemer, and that Joseph Smith was His prophet, that will save you and me, but it is the keeping of the commandments of God, the living the life of a Latter-day Saint.[1]

When I was a young mother living in Bountiful, Utah, there were terrible mudslides within a block of my home. One night we heard a loud sound, like a big train plowing a path without tracks. Mud came down from the mountain, taking the homes and property in its way. We had no water or electricity for two weeks. Helicopters flew overhead repeatedly, and the National Guard policed our area. Unless you lived there or were helping with the relief effort, you weren't allowed in that part of town.

I remember calling my mother, who lived in Arizona, to tell her we were okay. I knew it would be on national television and I didn't want her to worry. When I got a hold of her and told her what was happening, she said, "Oh, you'll be okay. You know what to do." Then she rehearsed a few basic emergency steps about water and light-heartedly reminded me again that I knew what to do and that I could handle it. It was true, and because we had our food storage, we didn't have to worry about getting to the grocery store right away either. We had followed counsel and were prepared.

We do our part even when we don't feel like it, even when it seems we're just going through the motions. My husband's great-grandmother, Mary Ann Simmons Smith, had an experience that exemplifies this kind of doing. Here is her experience written by her daughter, Mina May Smith Ovard.

> Mother's health was not at all what it should be, and at this particular time she was very sick. She had faith that if she would fast and go to fast meeting and be administered to, she would be blessed. The fast meetings those days were held on Thursday morning each month at eleven o'clock. This Thursday morning was very stormy, which prevented Mother from going. She was so disappointed she cried.

> Shortly after Mother had gone to bed that night discouraged, three women clothed in white appeared in the doorway. They came to her bedside and placed their hands upon her head and blessed her. She could feel their heavenly influence although she did not hear them speak. The next morning she felt well and strong and went about her work singing songs of praise to her Heavenly Father.

Mary Ann fasted even when she didn't feel like it. She had faith that her fasting would benefit her. President Howard W. Hunter said: "If our lives and our faith are centered on Jesus Christ and his restored gospel, nothing can ever go permanently wrong. On the other hand, if our lives are not centered on the Savior and his teachings, no other success can ever be permanently right."[2]

This pattern of *doing* works for the young and for the old. It is a continual process, aided by habits formed early in life. I'm reminded of a devoted daughter of God, Bessie McCarrel Hansen. I'm not sure how old Bessie was when she moved into our branch. When she passed away, she was 95 years old. Every Sunday I went to her room to take her to church. Every Wednesday I returned to take her to Relief Society. And every time I went to get her she thanked me profusely saying, "Thank you so much for coming to get me. I couldn't have gone without you. It means a lot to me." She must have repeated herself five times before I'd get her from her room to the meeting location. Although Bessie was in poor health, she never missed attending her meetings.

I noticed others in our branch who used their ailments as an excuse to stay in their apartments. Even though I offered to push them in their wheelchairs, some chose to make no effort to go. Oh, I know they experienced difficult times, but from my perspective it was more a matter of giving up the will to do—the mind and heart—rather than the body's failure. Their problems weren't any more difficult than Bessie's.

Our Relief Society presidency visited Bessie in her apartment one afternoon. We mentioned to her how grateful we were that she always attended her meetings. She said emphatically, "That is where I belong! Unless my body absolutely will not allow it, that is where I will be!"

It is people like Bessie who we see at our meetings every week—those who are steadfast and immovable in being obedient to God's command—who are willing to take and fulfill assignments. The same people consistently participate in lessons and bear their testimonies. These individuals are simply committed no matter what, and they never give up.

On the other hand, the gift of the Atonement gives us all hope. It is never too late to adopt the doing pattern. Another sister, Anna Butterfield, age 92, came to our branch a little unsteady in her commitment. As the sisters in our branch reached out to her and taught her, she too joined us for every meeting. And as she caught the Spirit, she wanted it all. She wanted to learn and understand the scriptures. She wanted her patriarchal blessing. She wanted to make temple covenants. Along with her home teacher, I had the privilege of teaching Anna the temple preparation lessons. What a thrill it was to watch her "wax strong in knowledge of the truth."

Having not paid tithing, Anna waited a few months to prove her worthiness by being consistent in her offering. Paying tithing is a requirement to securing for ourselves the safety ordinances of the temple.

In a General Conference talk in October 2005, Elder Henry B. Eyring said he understood it took time to learn to control spending with faith that what we have comes from God. He said he knew it took faith to pay tithing promptly and without procrastination. But he resolutely declared that if we would decide to be full-tithe payers and be steady in paying it, we would receive blessings throughout the year—we would be strengthened in our faith, our hearts would be softened, and we could be confident that we would qualify for protection in the last days.

When I was a single mom, I saw many miracles that I attributed to paying my tithing. Overnight, I became the provider.

Money was extremely scarce and hard to stretch far enough to care for my family and pay the bills. Up to that point, I'd been a full-tithe payer my whole life. In my dire circumstance, however, I questioned whether I could continue. I read in the scriptures the promises regarding paying tithes and consciously decided I would test that principle. I went to the Lord in prayer with this scripture in mind: "I, the Lord, am bound when ye do what I say; but when ye do not what I say, ye have no promise" (D&C 82:10).

In my prayer, I said something like this, "Heavenly Father, you've made these promises and you're bound in keeping them if I do my part. So I'm going to do my part completely and I expect your help to see me through." It wasn't a very conventional prayer, but it was a firm commitment on my part!

There were some extremely difficult times during those years. We didn't have the money for luxuries, but I saw miraculous intervention in acquiring jobs and seeing money stretch. On one occasion after the food storage was depleted, I got a phone call from a friend who had moved to another state and was unaware of our circumstances. She asked if she and her family could come and spend Easter weekend. She had older children with big appetites and I couldn't figure out how I could possibly feed them. I only had a few foodstuffs on the shelf as it was. But I decided to have faith that the Lord would help me help her. So I said, "Yes."

The day before my friend arrived with her family, we received an anonymous gift of bags full of groceries on our doorstep—enough to feed us all for the weekend and some time beyond. To this day I don't know who brought the food, but with all my heart I know God sustained me by keeping His promises in full.

And now, I, Moroni, would speak somewhat concerning

these things; I would show unto the world that faith is things which are hoped for and not seen; wherefore, dispute not because ye see not, for ye receive no witness until after the trial of your faith. (Ether 12:6)

I believed the scriptures. I chose to have faith, act on that faith (pay my tithing), and trust in the promises being kept. And I immediately began receiving confirmations that paying tithing was a true principle. With all the bizarre and scary things that happened during those years, I was blessed with comfort and peace and the assurance that my Father would see me through. And He did!

> I would that ye should remember, that as much as ye shall put your trust in God even so much ye shall be delivered out of your trials, and your troubles, and your afflictions, and ye shall be lifted up at the last day. (Alma 38:5)

Of course, being a full-tithe payer is not the only requirement to enter the temple. We must be temple worthy. Why is being temple worthy so important to our personal safety? And what does it mean to be temple worthy?

Here is the answer to the first question: Qualifying to enter the temple is the ultimate step in securing our peace, our protection, and our safety. In temples, we are instructed and receive the saving ordinances that provide sacred, eternal, and protective blessings. We receive:

- Increased personal revelation.

- Greater spiritual knowledge and power.

- Specific promises from Heavenly Father. Similar to paying tithing, He is bound if we keep our part of the covenant.

- The blessing of being sealed to families for time and eternity.

- The opportunity to unselfishly serve others.

And what do we have to do to qualify? We must:

- Have a testimony of Heavenly Father, of the Lord Jesus Christ, and of the Holy Ghost.

- Sustain the Lord's prophet and Church leaders.

- Faithfully attend sacrament meeting and other Church meetings.

- Strive to keep the Lord's commandments, including being honest in our dealings.

- Live a morally clean life and keep the Word of Wisdom.

- Act in harmony with the teachings of the Church.

During the Frankfurt Germany Temple dedication, President Ezra Taft Benson expressed his personal feelings about the power that comes from worthy temple attendance. He said when he was weighed down by problems or difficulties and went to the house of the Lord with a prayer in his heart for answers, those answers came in clear and unmistakable ways. He promised that, with increased attendance in the temples of our God, we shall receive increased personal revelation to bless our lives as we bless those who have died.

In regards to receiving protection, Elder Boyd K. Packer said there was no work we could do that could give us more power, nor was there any work that required a higher standard of righteousness. If we would accept the revelation concerning temple ordinance work and enter into our covenants without reservation or apology, Elder Packer said the Lord would protect us and we would receive inspiration sufficient for the challenges of life. Elder Packer invited us to come to the temple—come and claim our blessings.

I love that phrase—"come and claim our blessings." It's up to us. We make the choice.

Stephanie L. Yates expressed her joy in temple attendance by telling me the following:

> An elderly brother in our ward shared an experience about attending the temple. He had numerous health problems and had attended the temple the previous week. He said before he entered the temple that day he touched the outside wall. He said he had touched it to leave all his problems and worries in that very spot, to pick them back up on his way home. He completely forgot his worries in the temple that day, and, on the way out, forgot to pick them back up.
>
> I tried this. It works! Every time I now enter the temple, I touch the outside wall, leave my problems out there, and have a marvelous spiritual experience.

Sister Patricia T. Holland, wife of Elder Jeffrey R. Holland, shares the following personal experience, expanding on one of the reasons why temple worthiness is so important to our safety.

> My habit of looking for sacred symbols and my testimony of finding answers to personal problems were passed on from mother to daughter to granddaughter to me. I have learned through generations of Eve's daughters the very close connection between our temporal challenges and the spiritual world, and how one assists the other as it pertains to those who attend the temple. So that you will understand my deep feelings about this, I have chosen to share my first experience about the temple's sustaining power.
>
> I was twelve years old, living in Enterprise, Utah, when my parents were called to be temple workers in the St. George Temple, fifty miles away. In telling me of their call, my mother spoke to me of what temples were, why people serve there, and what spiritual experiences some of the saints have

had there. Certainly she believed that the seen and unseen worlds meet and mingle in the temple. My duties were to get excused early from school once a week and hurry home to tend five unruly brothers, the youngest of whom was just a toddler. I remember complaining about this assignment one day, and I will never forget the power with which my mother said, "When Daddy and I were set apart for this assignment, we were promised that our family would be blessed and protected, even by 'attending angels.'"

Late one afternoon on one of my parents' temple days, when I was feeling particularly exhausted from providing entertainment for my young charges, I put the baby in a buggy and, with the other boys, walked five blocks to visit with my grandmother.

After a warm greeting, Grandma suggested that we play on the lawn while she went to the store for refreshments. I was distracted with the other children and didn't notice the baby beginning to toddle after his grandmother. Suddenly, and with great fear, I realized that he was out of sight. Instinctively I ran toward the car just in time to see the back wheel turn completely over his small head, crushing it into the gravel beneath. In panic I screamed at the top of my lungs. My grandmother felt the distinct bump, heard my scream, and knew exactly what had happened. However, instead of stopping the car, she panicked and drove back over him again. Twice the wheel of the car moved completely over the head of this beloved baby brother for whom I had been given full responsibility.

The wailing of two hysterical voices quickly caught the attention of my grandfather. He dashed from the house and gathered up the baby (who my grandmother and I were sure was dead), and the three of them frantically drove fifty miles to the nearest doctor. I prayed and cried—cried and prayed. However, children remember promises made even when adults might forget, and I was curiously calm and comforted. I remembered the part about "attending angels."

After what seemed like an eternity, my grandparents called and reported that the baby was fine. He had a badly scratched face where the tire had scraped his head and cheek, but there was no cranial damage. Yet twice I had clearly seen the force of that wheel on his head.

At age twelve one cannot know many spiritual things. I especially did not know what went on in the temple of God. But I knew from my experience that it was sacred, and that hovering near, with approval and protection, were heavenly angels. I knew something of heavenly help beyond the veil.

In Doctrine and Covenants 109, that section which teaches us of the holiness of the temple, verse 22 reads: "We ask thee, Holy Father, that thy servants may go forth from this house armed with thy power, and that thy name may be upon them, and thy glory be round about them, and thine angels have charge over them."

That is a powerful promise to those who feel over-whelmed with the pressures and stresses of daily living, a power and promise I first encountered at twelve years of age. Now, with the many experiences I have had since that age, I can declare that this is true. The temple provides protection and it provides patterns and promises that can settle and strengthen and stabilize us, however anxious our times.[3]

Darlene Forbes (introduced in the previous chapter) recently met a man she believes understands and values the gospel as she does. But because of past experiences, she found herself once again confused and questioning . . . not for the same reasons as before, however. There were no glaring red flags, but the cir-cumstances were difficult to decipher. She went to the temple and prayed for answers. She told the Lord she was seeking a man

who would make and keep sacred covenants, one who understood his role in an eternal partnership and would be intentional
about his responsibilities in the family, one who would treat her
with respect and honor. When she got home, she grabbed her
journal, as before, and wrote down the answers she received in
the temple. This is how she explained it to me:

> If you picture a circle or a pie with slices, the smallest
> piece of the pie is "Things I Know That I Know" (example:
> I have blonde hair, I am a daughter of God, etc.). A slightly
> larger piece of the pie is "Things I Know That I Don't
> Know" (quantum physics, the intelligence of a rock, etc.).
> The majority of the pie, or the largest slice, is "Things That I
> Don't Know That I Don't Know." I have no examples of this
> because I don't know what I don't know! But I'm aware I have
> that big slice, especially in those moments when I hear myself
> responding to something with, "I never knew that!"

So these are some of the things I felt confident about
while in the temple.

1. I should be patient and "stay the course."

2. I am endowed with power to get through this.

3. I should talk to my bishop.

So I find myself liking this man more and more every
time we talk, and my heart is getting involved more than is
comfortable for me. So even though I have my answer and
know what I am to do, the Lord has asked me to do something I would rather not do—be patient. I want to run. He
says to stay. So I stay.

So this is my list of things that I know that I know, without a doubt.

1. I am being obedient to the inspiration I received in the
temple.

2. I will know God a little better when I am through this.

3. I can survive any heartbreak that comes my way.

4. I am going to be an amazing wife and have a great marriage one day.

5. Everything is going to be okay.

I am hoping the things I know that I know will give me the strength to overcome the things I know that I don't know and the things that I don't know that I don't know!

Although Darlene's situation is a "work in progress," I will tell you a little more in the next chapter. It is enough at this point, however, to note her tenacity in clinging to the fifth thread of power and safety—to learn and consistently obey the commandments of God.

NOTES:

1. President Heber J. Grant, "The President Speaks," *Improvement Era*, Nov. 1936, 659.

2. President Howard W. Hunter, in *The Teachings of Howard W. Hunter*, ed. Clyde J. Williams (Salt Lake City: Deseret Book, 1997), 40.

3. Jeffrey R. Holland, Patricia T. Holland, *On Earth As It Is in Heaven* (Salt Lake City: Deseret Book, 1989), 63–65.

CHAPTER 7

Goal Setting

—◦◦◦◦—

All victory and glory is brought to pass unto you through your diligence, faithfulness, and prayers of faith.
—D&C 103:36

—◦◦◦◦—

Elder Richard G. Scott told a large-capacity crowd at Brigham Young University that when temptations come, individuals are given strength beyond their own capacity if they have taken a determined stand for right, established personal standards, and made covenants to keep them. He said the difficulty comes when individuals enter the battle of temptation without a fixed plan.

Remember the story from the previous chapter about Darlene? Her story shows us the power and truth of Elder Scott's words. From the start, Darlene entered the battle with a fixed plan—be temple worthy and steadfast in leaning on the Lord.

One of my daughters recently sent me pictures from her excursion to Hiroshima, Japan, the place where the dreaded atomic bomb fell. One picture showed a surviving willow tree. It was about a half mile from the epicenter. Many strips of brown tape were wrapped around the trunk to hold it securely together, and the branches were held up by heavy, wooden props, but it lives—a symbol of perseverance in spite of tragedy. It made me think of early pioneer women who experienced such extreme hardships, women of today in countries where womanhood is still not respected or esteemed, and modern-day pioneer women, like Darlene, who battle intense trials in our day. And through it all, we persevere in spite of our hard times. We gain strength and an increased capacity to handle what comes because we cling to our values and keep our covenants.

I'm blessed to live fairly close to a temple. On my walk, I can look up the street and beyond, to the foothills, and see the temple. From my perspective, the temple resembles a lighthouse or beacon on the nearby hill. Like the willow tree, the temple is a symbol of perseverance in a world filled with chaos. President Thomas S. Monson said the temple is a refuge from life's storms. He said temples were like never-failing beacons guiding us to safety.

Considering our circumstances, we can set specific goals to help us enter our battles with a fixed plan.

We've all heard it said, "Your actions speak louder than your words." Well, it's true. Our standards, our integrity, even our willingness to conform to God's will are reflected in how we process our thoughts and use our available time. Everything we do, whether it is a task or just a thought, takes time. We control the outcome of our lives by controlling our time.

We won't reach our goals overnight, but we'll have increased peace knowing we are making the conscious choice to not simply drift along in the hope that life places us on the right path and faces us in the right direction. With a "do it" attitude we can think things through and determine what we're aiming for. Next, we can step back and figure out what manageable steps we're going to take to get there. Then we can set realistic timetables and take action.

Many years ago, in an effort to keep physically fit, I ran in a two-mile race just prior to a scheduled 10K. I huffed and panted, walking a good part of the distance. Yet I finished and was satisfied until I stood at the sidelines watching the runners gather for the 10K starting gun. I thought, *"Are they all crazy?"* They were going to run over six miles, yet they stood chattering excitedly with anticipation like a flock of Canadian "honkers" ready for their spring flight north. I didn't stay to see the finish. I just shook my head and walked away believing they were making a mistake to push themselves so hard.

Three of my children joined me on that two-mile run. Later in the week, as we talked about it, one of them commented, "You know, the six-mile would only be like running three of the two-mile!"

I'd never thought of it like that. It occurred to me that if I practiced and committed myself, in time, I probably could do three two-mile runs. I didn't dare voice that thought, but the seed of challenge was planted, and I wanted to see if I could do it!

I promised myself I'd run five days a week, three miles a day for the next year. And I did it. I ran in the rain . . . in the snow . . . in the heat. I set up a daily schedule and developed it into a habit. I arose early to read, then did warm-up exercises and calisthenics for half an hour. Afterward I ran my three miles and thought about what I'd read, where my priorities were, and what I wanted to do about them.

After a year I realized it was my vision that had been short, not my potential. I committed to another year of the same conditioning and then voiced my goal. As my family sat at the dinner table, I announced my decision to enter the 10K. Then turning to my son, who was almost sixteen, I asked, "Marcus, will you run with me in the race?"

"How far's that?" he questioned with an I-don't-think-I-want-to-be-involved look.

I replied, "6.2 miles."

"I don't know, Mom. That's a long way," he said shaking his head.

"If you work at it, it could help you with your endurance and speed for football. Will you?" I asked again.

"Well I guess so," came the quiet reply.

"Is that a yes?"

"Yeah." And there it was, my committed goal stated and Marcus's too! The next eleven months I paced my running to shorten my time per mile, and increased the distance. I included bicycling in my weekly workout, giving me variety and building different muscles. As I increased my distance, I realized I could have met my goal sooner if I had only conceived it earlier. It wasn't any harder to run four miles now than it had been to run three. It was all a matter of mind-set. (I have to admit today there seems to be a bit more than mind set involved—as my body has aged, I don't know if it is the will that is lacking or simply the capacity!)

It was about 90 degrees with 70% humidity as I did my practice runs that last week before the race. I had to break down the distance in my mind by setting landmarks along the roadside to keep me going. *"I just can't go any faster,"* I thought. I was pushing myself so hard I wasn't enjoying the road along the way anymore. I wanted so much to win—to be the best. But that wasn't my original goal. It had been to pace my training to enable me to finish a 10K. And now it wasn't my best I was after; I wanted the praise and glory of being the winner.

Race day brought cooler weather. The sound of the gun was muffled by the "honking" around me. The flock began moving forward. The air of excitement was so thick it took my breath away without me lifting a foot. I was at the rear, but ever so slowly I inched my way forward. By the third mile I came upon my football-player son, obviously struggling to continue, his pride and determination pushing him on. It was a thrill for me to pass him! By the end of the fourth mile I was really hurting too and was so consumed with tension I couldn't exercise what I'd learned in training.

During those previous weeks of painful practice runs, I found relief from conscious discomfort by thinking about someone or something other than myself. I thought about solutions to problems like what I could do for the children or my husband, or how I could cheer someone or thank another.

But during the race my muscles would not be consoled. The breathing of the flock was so concentrated, the pounding of foot to pavement so determined, I couldn't think beyond the effort of lifting one foot in front of the other. At the fifth mile I honestly didn't care who won. I just wanted it to be over! I tried to remember my goal, my commitment, and determined I was not going to quit. Even if I had to crawl, I would not give up. Ah, I could see the finish line, the crowd cheering. I looked for my time . . . slower than I'd hoped. Then I was over the finish line. With tears of satisfaction I met my goal—*my* goal. I did my best.

My thoughts immediately went to Marcus and I began running back to find him. He had not stopped. He said he hurt so intensely he wanted to throw up! But he had kept his commitment to finish the race. We both came across the finish line and then walked in shuffles, bent over with our hands on our hips. Within minutes my family was around us, lending congratulations. We ate oranges and visited with the other runners until awards were given.

We cheered with pride when Marcus was awarded the second place trophy for males age 15–19. The winner of my age category crossed the line 14 minutes before me. Oh, it made me tired just thinking about it. "What's that?" I thought as I heard them award the second place trophy to a woman who had run over the finish line literally steps in front of me. My name was called . . . third. "Imagine that!" I said to myself. "If I had gathered just enough reserve to put a little kick in right at the end, I could have made second place! With a little more training I'll bet I could do it . . ." And there it was—another goal in the making!

I mention this experience because it is so true to most things that happen to us in life. First, we rationalize our level of performance and criticize those who do more than we do. Second, if we open our eyes and it's something we want, we see that if we cut the elephant into bite-size pieces, so to speak, we can eat the elephant too. (Maybe for animal lovers that is a bad analogy!) And third, we all have a reserve we're not aware of and are capable of so much more than we think we are.

I've run a lot of races since then and earned my share of first-place trophies and ribbons, but the fact of the matter is that if I hadn't had a desire to take care of my body and improve my physical fitness, I wouldn't have taken that first walk. If I hadn't set my sights to achieve a little more and been willing to move out of my comfort zone, I wouldn't have won that first trophy and realized I had the potential to do more. If I hadn't set a goal and paced out a plan and then worked that plan with zeal, I would never have enjoyed the thrill of hitting one of my targets.

I'm not saying that running a race was a goal I had to achieve to fulfill my mission in life. I'm just saying that it was one of those milestone experiences that helped me grow. It was one of those experiences I was able to learn from and build upon. Among other things, through that process, I learned that when I feel overwhelmed with my challenges and want to give up, or that I can't keep up the pace anymore, I need to slow down, not quit. It doesn't all have to be done today. I can keep hope and relax a little until the energy builds to pick up the pace again, always reaching for the best that is in me, not comparing myself to someone else or setting myself up to be better than another. I need to excel in competition only with myself.

I never thought I would have the experiences I've had in life. They have not been what I could have conceived. But looking back on my life, I can see divine intervention and a choreography I cannot explain. However, if I had not reached out of my comfort zone to meet new goals along the way, my life might have taken a completely different path. And my experiences or times of seeming failure have probably been some of the most instrumental of my life, because they prepared me for greater experiences and events to come.

No matter what others may say, our futures don't just happen. We actually invent our futures by our personal choices. Even when our circumstances seem to narrow our options—such as when our health is poor or when we are single and sole providers for our families—we must not give up. We must keep a clear perspective of our divine purpose and believe that changes in our lives are just challenges, not threats. And we must focus on what we can control in finding solutions to those challenges.

Indulge me by doing this simple exercise. Take a minute and imagine staring into an elegant, two-sided, magic mirror. The mirror not only provides a reflection but also allows the perception of thought. One side of the mirror is framed in a rich, reddish-brown mahogany, like the wood used for making tasteful furniture. The other side of the mirror has a pearly-white, enamel frame adorned with silky, soft floral in all the beautiful colors of nature.

Look into the mirror side framed in mahogany. See your image aged to 95 years, lying very still on the bed and soon gracefully to pass on to the next life and meet family and friends.

Perceive your thoughts, reviewing and evaluating what you've accomplished in this mortal existence, and how you will be remembered. Let's say you have followed the same path you're on in reality right now—the same priorities, the same choices of the use of your time. Looking into the mirror, showing you at 95 years, would you perceive happy contentment or wishes for different choices in your life?

Turn the mirror over. Look into the joyfully decorated, white-framed side. In this side of the mirror see yourself in a moving picture of time, accomplishing your dreams and your divine purpose. See yourself confidently participating in daily activities that reflect charity, service, and integrity. Perceive a feeling of inner peace because you are following God's plan for you.

How do we match the reminiscent reflections on the mahogany side to the likeness on the pearly-white side? Is there anything we need to do now, in reality, to change our priorities, the choices of the use of our time, to make it possible for our vision at 95 years to be hopeful and happy? Perhaps we should take a completely different path or direction than what we are presently pursuing. Or maybe there is something we do well but with a concerted effort could do a little better. Are we working our schedules around what is truly important rather than trying to work what is important into our schedules?

Remember, we control the outcome of our lives by controlling our time. We have to allow the leverage of purposely setting goals—goals that fulfill our dreams and our divine purpose, like the reflection in the mirror. And then we can plan time now, pacing ourselves to the finish, just like running a race, so we'll accomplish our goals with our personal priorities in place.

If we need to change our path or pattern of living to accomplish those goals, we are going to have to be willing to leave our comfort zones. It's always going to be easier to do what's familiar—what we are used to. And even though that familiar thing may not be healthy, or get us to the finish line we're after, we do it because it is comfortable and we don't have to think about it or put in much effort.

Some time ago I went running with a friend. In our conversation after the run, she said she was very careful about the shoes she wore so the cushion would protect her knees and back. I knew it was about time for me to get new shoes, but I hadn't wanted to spend the time to check mine out or spend the money on new ones. That evening I took a good look at my shoes and was amazed what poor condition they were in. I had run a hole in the toe. The center tread of the ball of the shoe was nearly worn through. And because I pronate, the outside of the heel was worn down. I might as well have been running in my socks! But I was used to it. The feel of the run was *familiar*.

My daughter and I happened to be in the shopping mall a few days later and I stepped into the shoe store to check on the price of new running shoes. There was a terrific salesman there who set me up with the most cushiony shoes, and, being the only running shoes left in the store that were my size, I paid the price. That was a Saturday.

The following Monday I was really excited about going out with my new shoes. I got up early and eagerly started my run. Those new shoes had air pockets in the heels. My feet and legs weren't used to having this extra bounce, let alone full tread. So I spent more time in the air than I did putting distance behind me. The shoes felt so different from what I was used to that they threw me off balance. By the time I ran three miles, I was hobbling.

The second day went the same way. I wanted to return the shoes and wear my old ones. Even though the new shoes, in the long run, would be healthier for me, I longed for the *familiar* feeling of being in control of where my feet were going! That day I purposely threw the old ones in the garbage because I knew they presented too much temptation for me to return to my old ways.

We have to stick with it. We have to be willing to run the risk of being uncomfortable for a while. *We have to make the good thing feel familiar before it can feel good.* It took me a couple weeks, but I finally got control of my shoes!

Of course most life changes are bigger or take more time than new shoes. Break the bigger challenges into pieces and pace them out. Even little, focused modifications can direct us toward our goals. We have the agency of choice. We are not accountable for anyone else's mission. We are responsible for *our* missions. Regardless of what has brought us to this point, whatever our circumstances, the Lord will bless us with the strength we need if we have faith and put in the effort.

Our attitude and our vision make a tremendous difference in how we see and respond to our circumstances and the outcome of our lives. So many doubts and fears conspire to keep us from changing for the better. Sometimes the hardest part of change is believing we have the personal power to bring about that change. And sometimes we just can't see how to find a realistic starting point. We can start with a willingness to come out of our comfort zone and take the risk of making life better for ourselves.

We spend time in our mind in either our area of concern or our area of influence. The more time we spend in our area of concern—which is worrying about things we have no control over—the more powerless we feel. The more time we spend in our area of influence—which is acting, or reacting to things we can have some level of control over—the more we are going to feel a sense of personal power and accountability about the choices we make. We become a catalyst for change in that environment. As we do things within our control on a daily basis, our area of influence grows.

Our view of our circumstances and our self-image may or may not be in line with reality. It may be merely what we have accepted. Many of us fool even ourselves by the role we play. But sooner or later we come to question our itinerary along the pathway of life. Sooner or later we want to believe what we are doing is important—we want to have a sense of purpose, of faith in what we're doing.

Finding our reality does not come without a plan or effort. First, we have to find out who we are and what we really believe. Then we need to live by what we believe and not be swayed by what we simply have accepted of ourselves. We can consciously choose our destination and believe in our ability to learn and move forward. And we must not measure what we are or where we are going by looking at others or by looking at where we've been.

Goals can provide us with a clear sense of purpose, an objective, a plan. When we set goals and accomplish them, we feel more in control. Since written goals are realized far more often than those that remain only in thought or verbalized, we can think of what we saw looking into the pearly-white side of the mirror, and write down on paper three specific things we can do to work toward making that imagined reflection a reality.

When I followed this little exercise, my first thought was that I wanted to recommit to gaining more knowledge, particularly more knowledge of Christ and his gospel and how to apply it in my life. Second, I wanted my husband and my children to know that I love them. Third, I wanted to pace the activities of my life better so I didn't feel like a scrambled egg as often! These "I want . . ." statements became the basis of my written goals.

We can take our "I want . . ." statements and reword them as though we have already achieved them. I rewrote mine as follows:

1. I am gaining more knowledge, particularly more knowledge of Christ and his gospel and how to apply it in my life.

2. My husband and my children know I love them.

3. I pace the activities of my life to avoid the scrambled-egg syndrome.

Now we have three written goals. Some of them may be short-term, others long-term. Where possible, date the goals. If one of my goals had been to be in shape, for instance, to run a 10K, I would have written the date of the 10K as a part of my written goal. For this exercise, however, my goals each pertained to an everyday desired result. So I rewrote them as follows:

1. On this day I am gaining more knowledge, particularly more knowledge of Christ and his gospel and how to apply it now.

2. Today my husband and my children know I love them.

3. I am pacing my activities today to avoid the scrambled-egg syndrome.

What are we going to do to achieve our goals? Be specific, and write it down in as few words as possible so it can be read and reviewed quickly and easily.

1. On this day I am gaining more knowledge, particularly more knowledge of Christ and his gospel and how to apply it now by doing the following:
    • Each morning, I pray for God's influence that I may learn and develop His attributes and that my mission

be made clear to me—that He reveal to me my part in His plan.

- I attend my church meetings regularly and prepare appropriately to fulfill my church callings.

- I attend the temple once a month.

- I read at least one verse from the scriptures each evening before I go to bed.

- Each evening, I pray for God's influence that I may understand the scriptures and know how they pertain to me.

Note that my first goal is fully within my control, my area of influence. It is all a matter of my putting in the effort. There are a lot of options I could write down pertaining to this goal. However, these are the ones that fit me now. As time passes and seasons change in my life, I might select different options to achieve that goal. But look at my second goal, "Today my husband and my children know I love them." Can I really control that? No, because they have their agency, and I cannot control their feelings or perceptions. Wanting my husband and my children to know I love them is in my area of concern. However, I *can* control how *I feel* and what *I do* to show my love. That is in my area of influence. I can do things that will most likely generate the feeling of being loved (if they are presented honestly). And as I focus on what I presently have control of, I can positively influence the outcome. In this case my area of influence might even grow to include our friends, our neighbors, and those we work with.

2. Today my husband and my children know I love them because:

- I pray for them each day and ask Heavenly Father to help them feel my love.

- I tell them I love them and touch them with a hug or shoulder squeeze when I am with them.

- I listen and look at them when they speak to me.

- I catch them doing things right and tell them so.

- I advise them when asked, but let them make their own decisions, and I honor those decisions.

- I call on the telephone and visit with my children that live out of town at least once a month (not just Internet messaging—I attempt to reach them by phone so I can hear the tone of their voices and sense their feelings behind their words).

- I devote each Friday evening as a date-night with my husband.

Those who know me probably laughed when reading my third goal. I always seem to overextend myself. But remember—goals are not based on what a person has or has not done in the past. They are based on what a person wants to do, what she wants to become, and in this case, how I want to behave.

Because I am a woman, because I am a wife, because I am a mother, because I like to do everything and thus have multiple demands on my time, this third goal is probably my most difficult goal to achieve: "I am pacing my activities today to avoid the scrambled-egg syndrome." Like the second goal, it is both in my area of concern and my area of influence. I cannot control when my daughter is going to call me from the hospital asking me to drop everything and come for my grandson, her first son, because her second son needs immediate treatment and she can't handle them both. But I can control how I act in response to that request. And knowing that my problem has more often been that I expected myself to do too much, not that I had too much to do, I can concentrate on scheduling more reasonably and adapting more freely.

3. I am pacing my activities today to avoid the scrambled-egg syndrome by:

- Each Friday, using my calendar book (or other form of calendaring), I plan the following week, picking up those items not completed the week before and using caution to not over-book myself for activities on any given day.

- Each morning I check my calendar book (or other form of calendaring) to prepare an effective and realistic timeline for completing the tasks of the day.

- I allow more time when a task involves working with other people.

- I put a higher priority on tasks and events that help me achieve my first two goals.

- Each day I act instead of feeling guilty or verbally reacting.

- Each day I remember it is temporary when the events of my day become out of control—this too will pass. I accept it, reevaluate, and reschedule.

Once we've written our goal statements, we put them in a place where we can review them often, at least once a day. We rewrite them, if necessary, to clarify them and make them a way of thinking, believing, and then acting. We can use our calendar book (or other system) to formulate a schedule that dates checkpoints to achieve our goals. At least once a week, as we review our goals, we consciously look at our behavior to see if it matches our goals. When we evaluate how our goals and our behavior match up, we can recognize the progress we've made instead of the distance still ahead. We can relax and move confidently forward if we plan and follow that plan.

Sometimes the route we choose to accomplish a goal doesn't move us forward. And what may be important to us today may not be so significant tomorrow. As we grow, we need to be flexible. We can reevaluate what we want and how we want to get it. Write it down and act on it. If it works, do it some more. If it doesn't work, we can determine where we are now, what went right or wrong, and why. We can look for other options to accomplish the desired outcome. We need to give ourselves the liberty to develop our personal power. If we have established realistic, attainable goals, over time, with a consistent effort, we will attain most of them.

We usually begin a project like this with enthusiasm, belief, and energy, but seeing our goals through to completion is another matter. Too often the vision of what we can accomplish dissipates as our time and abilities are challenged. We've got to believe in ourselves and put the past behind us and start each day with a clean slate of self-expectancy. We can dwell on our positive qualities and use them to our best advantage while using our strengths to help achieve our goals. We can decide to be happy and hopeful by replacing frustration and worry with action planning. Most of our limits are self-imposed and don't reflect our real ability nor our real capacity. We can reject the fear of failure and have the courage to act on our individual purpose.

When we develop the habit of choosing our responses to life's experiences, we make ourselves a product of our decisions instead of our conditions. We can simplify the things that don't really matter, and organize ourselves so we gain control of our day. When frustration seems endless, despite our degree of effort, we can go back to the level where we felt successful.

When we return to a level where something feels easy, we regain enthusiasm and confidence.

When we set goals and achieve them, we gain a sense of value and respect for ourselves, and we feel more in control of our lives. But we shouldn't be afraid to experience the richness of the process of accomplishing those goals. Achieving the end goal is simply a by-product of developing a healthy, vibrant, resourceful lifestyle. We achieve our unique purposes in life by reflecting on the past, having the vision of tomorrow, and acting today.

The sixth thread of power and safety is to steadily pace our efforts so we can endure and meet with a strong finish our goal of becoming a daughter of God.

CHAPTER 8

Supporting Each Other

—❦—

This is my commandment, That ye love one another, as I have loved you.
—John 15:12

—❦—

Not long ago, Darlene Forbes called me on the telephone. She was suffering from post-traumatic stress disorder and asked for my advice. I listened for a while as she explained what was happening and what she was doing to cope. Then I said, "Darlene, you're doing all the right things." I identified for her the pattern she routinely follows when life is difficult. I said, "Trust that you're going to be okay. If you continue to follow that pattern, in time, all will come out right for you." We talked a little longer, and I assured her she was on the right path and encouraged her to stay with it.

We both had experienced true trauma and knew the value of friendship to talk it out, lift us up, and help us carry on. But we agreed our real success had come from making the choice to rely on the Lord. Knowing our every action starts with a thought, I suggested she write a goal she could read to herself every day, one that would settle her thinking on the positive and give her reason to believe she was safe.

That evening, after our conversation, I thought about my own feelings of safety and how I weathered difficult times. I wrote a goal for myself. The act of thinking it through and writing it down was helpful, but I knew reading it every day and honestly pondering it would continue to benefit me. This is the goal I wrote:

> Life is good because I trust my Heavenly Father. I know He is in charge. I am safe because I lean on the Holy Ghost to guide me. I carefully listen. I am lifted up and courageous in my thoughts and actions. I do my part and know assuredly Heavenly Father keeps His promises.

That conversation with Darlene was pivotal in writing this book. The pattern we discussed included certain powerful threads woven in the tapestry of our lives. As I mentioned in the introduction, as long as we do our part to consistently adhere life's experiences to those threads, come what may, they form a simple, proven pattern that guarantees success and safety. In previous chapters, I've presented six of the eight mighty threads that can strengthen, protect, and sustain each of us.

1. Recognizing our identity and acting with all our might to become daughters of God.

2. Leaning on the Lord with complete trust and doing our part to communicate with our Father through prayer.

3. Putting on the full armor of God by acting with faith and clinging to the scriptures.

4. Increasing our personal power of awareness.

5. Consistently obeying the commandments of God.

6. Steadily pacing our efforts so we can endure and meet with a strong finish our goal of becoming a daughter of God.

And here is the seventh thread:

7. Supporting each other in loving sisterhood.

One fall, I was juicing the grapes from our garden to make jelly. The process was very slow because I needed two hands for each step. I wondered why Heavenly Father created us with only two arms and hands. At the time I was thinking, *"Wouldn't it have been just as easy for him to design us each with four arms and hands so we could do things faster?"*

My daughter Angela was visiting with me in the kitchen while she watched. After a few minutes, she went to the kitchen sink and filled the colander with grapes and rinsed and drained them (step one). I was running grapes that I had already cleaned through the juicer (step two). When I finished step two, she handed me the colander prepared from step one. We talked and laughed as we finished the juicing process in half the time it would have taken me alone.

It occurred to me that if Heavenly Father had created us with four arms and hands, we wouldn't feel the joy and companionship that comes from serving others. We wouldn't learn the art of cooperation and teamwork. We would more often be loners and have fewer opportunities to talk and buoy each other up. It is not God's plan to isolate us. Being placed here on earth together offers us opportunities to be tested, to act as an obstacle or challenge, or to contribute to the solution and be a resource for others. We are on this earth together to work out our salvation.

The act of doing something for someone, whether it's through visiting teaching, community service, or just dinner to an ailing friend or neighbor can supply genuine satisfaction and joy. An associate of mine told me that whenever she complained to her friend about being depressed, her friend would say, "You need to take a dinner to someone!"

For most of us, it's more comfortable to be on the giving rather than the receiving end when it comes to supporting each other. But really the blessings flow both ways. Since no one, absolutely no one, sees life the same, we have the opportunity to lift up each other just by conveying a different perspective drawn from our experiences in mortality and before. Being women, we have an innate nurturing tendency. Even when life is hard for both, two women can lighten each other's load by listening, hugging, crying, or laughing together.

After my appendix surgery, I was placed in intensive care at the hospital, but I didn't respond well. Although I needed special care, it was determined I might do better in a regular room where I could have a roommate to talk to and where I could see outside through a window. I was moved to an area shared with a woman who had just undergone breast surgery. The tumor removed from her breast was benign. She was so elated her enthusiasm filled the room. Even with the tubes and pumps I was connected to, I couldn't help laughing at the jokes she made. She was Jewish and I a Mormon. Her rabbi came in and my bishop came in. We all laughed about the silliest, most nonsensical things. My condition steadily improved once I was placed in that room. We were both released from the hospital earlier than expected. I remember it was Christmas Eve and the hospital staff said we had to leave since we were making the other patients depressed because we were having so much fun! To this day I thank that hospital roommate for contributing to my good health with her companionship and contagious humor.

Because of life's experiences, in a week's time subtle changes happen to each of us. Today's fast-paced lifestyles tend to separate us, leaving us with few opportunities to laugh together, dream together, and develop philosophies together, unless we plan for it.

Some time ago, my cousin sent me a note telling me about a doctor friend. The friend had confided in my cousin about his mother-in-law who lived through the horrors of Nazi Germany and the invasion of Berlin. My cousin didn't elaborate on all the unbelievable things this woman had to witness and experience—being raped, watching her family die, having her home bombed, and so on. She told me that after the woman survived the war, she got a job with a businessman. He insisted on two-hour lunches. He also insisted that they eat quickly so the rest of their lunch time could be spent walking together. During their walks, he asked her over and over to tell him about her experiences and her feelings and her fears and anxieties. She said that was what saved her sanity—having someone to talk to that was willing to listen to the same things over and over and over.

The act of talking to someone we can safely air our concerns to is one of the most effective ways to work through trauma or grief.

My husband has an amazing ability to be patient and listen to me talk about the same things over and over. And I do appreciate his ever-loving, listening ear. However, it's a known fact that men and women see things from a different angle, and sometimes that (seemingly) nonsensical, female chitchat with a supportive friend could be labeled true therapy. One of my sisters lives approximately two hours distance from me. We plan a get-together about every three months just for that purpose—therapy! Because we share the same values, the same love of family, and the same eternal goals, we can talk and talk and talk (which means one is listening, listening, listening) for hours. We don't judge each other. We freely air our concerns, offer our opinions and suggestions, and inevitably go home with new insights, feeling like our burdens are lifted and we can manage life.

Of course, one of our closest friends should be the Holy Ghost. Being sensitive to the Spirit provides us with direction on how and when to help others, as well as what to do for our own well-being and safety.

Some of us will experience times when the Spirit seems to shout at us with warnings for our rescue. One of my dear friends, Lori Frischknecht, can testify of that. Her life was saved because of urgent directives given by the Spirit. Here is her story as she told it to me.

When I was about 14 or 15 years old, I played on a couple of softball teams. At the end of the season, we all decided to go out to Willard Bay to play in the water, picnic, and just enjoy the day. Several of us were playing Frisbee in the water. In the mid-1970s there was no such thing as water shoes or water socks. I could not stand the gooiness of the sand and moss between my toes. So I played in the water with an old pair of Converse tennis shoes. Yup, the big, heavy ones!

Someone tossed the Frisbee out far into the water. I was closest, so I swam out to get it. All of a sudden, the shoes felt incredibly heavy, and I started to go under. I frantically called to my friends. They all thought I was just playing around. So they did not pay much attention and turned away from me, saying things like, "Quit playing around," or "Not funny!" I began to really panic and was having a hard time keeping my head above the water. I realized that I indeed could drown out there.

Suddenly, a firm voice came from behind me and said, "Lori, turn on your back." I was so startled I actually looked behind me as my head came up. No one was there. I couldn't figure it out. Again, with more intensity, the voice said, "Lori, turn on your back." By this time, I did not question. I flipped on my back and floated in to shore. I was so shaken that I just stayed on the shore for quite awhile. It took some time for me to really grasp that my life had been saved by the Spirit speaking to me.

I have heard the Spirit speak to me in many different ways, but never with the urgency and power that I felt on that hot August day at Willard Bay.

On the other hand, some of us will experience times when the Spirit speaks in a soft, quiet tone to guide and protect us—a voice so faint we almost feel we have to reach out for it and bring it in close to examine and understand. Lori has experienced this type of communication also.

During the remodeling of our living room, we worked on it whenever we could. One night, we worked right through dinner. Later, we called a local pizza place to deliver some pizza, so we all could eat.

When the pizza came, I was busy with something. It took me a few minutes to write the check. Our girls answered the door. I could hear them chatting in the living room with the delivery person. As soon as I came around the corner into the living room, I was hit with an amazingly strong impression. Something felt wrong. I watched this young man speak to my girls, and I realized that he brought with him a very real and evil spirit into our home. I paid him quickly and sent him on his way.

Our oldest daughter, who was around twelve at the time, told me that she felt very uncomfortable around this man, and that she did not have a good feeling when he was in our home. I agreed with her. Our nine-year-old daughter told me later that the man scared her, even though he did nothing scary. As I got dinner on, I could not shake that horrible feeling. It was no longer present in our home, but it bothered

113

me and continued to worry me. I also realized that this man was extremely interested, in a horrible way, in our daughters. I began to pray that he would forget them, that his memory of them would be wiped from his mind.

For the next few days, I was still bothered by this experience. One of my dear friends "happened" to call. At the time, she was working as a 911 operator for Mesa, Arizona. I told her of the incident. Because it scared me so much, I was fervently hoping that she would say that I had blown the whole thing out of proportion, that I was over-tired, and that I was over-reacting and needed to move on. She did none of those things. In fact, she confirmed everything and more. She explained to me that because we are members of the Church, we know it to be the Holy Ghost, but she had seen this time and time again at work. People would say they had a bad feeling about a person or situation, that in fact, they had been warned. My friend explained that as 911 operators, they told people to pay attention to that "sixth sense" and not to dismiss it. She then told me to pay attention to strange cars that are spending time on my block, to call the police if this man showed up, and to have the children play in the backyard. I was even more afraid, and I wanted to protect my girls.

I prayed many times day and night that the man would forget our girls. I prayed for days, weeks, and months. I was very aware of my surroundings. Over time, the feeling left. I knew that my prayers had been answered. I also learned many lessons, specifically to pay attention and to trust myself and the Spirit when I felt in danger. We did not order pizza for a long time after that. But when we did, my husband or I met the person at the door with the money ready. I have never seen that particular man since then, and I am grateful. I am also grateful to have learned that when there is danger, the Spirit will let me know and I will listen.

Sometimes the Spirit warns someone else to come to our aid. Just prior to my divorce, when I felt alone, vulnerable, and scared—overcome with fear and nearly hopeless—my Relief Society president called. She said, "You've been on my mind. Is everything okay?" The bizarre events of my life at that time were full of intrigue, deceit, and mystery. Heavenly Father sent a compassionate person with ears to hear and hands to help. In addition, my faithful visiting teacher stepped in to assist.

These modern-day women pioneers were in tune with the Spirit and came in answer to my prayers. An early pioneer recorded the following when speaking about the spirit of sisterhood in Nauvoo: "The love of God flowed from heart to heart, till the wicked one seemed powerless in his efforts to get between us and the Lord, and his cruel darts, in some instances, were shorn of their sting."[1]

As we turn our hearts to each other, we act as God's hands in providing strength and relief. Sometimes all we need to find courage to face our troubles is a private, listening ear. Often, as in my meetings with my sister, when we have the opportunity to talk to a friend we trust, we feel hopeful and find ourselves coming up with and verbalizing our own solid solutions to our problems. Suffering dissolves and resiliency blooms when there is hope.

NOTE:
1. Helen Mar Whitney, "Scenes and Incidents at Winter Quarters," *Woman's Exponent*, vol. 14, no. 13, Dec. 1, 1885, 98.

CHAPTER 9

Patience

Verily I say unto you my friends, fear not, let your hearts be comforted; yea, rejoice evermore, and in everything give thanks; waiting patiently on the Lord, for your prayers have entered into the ears of the Lord of Sabaoth, and are recorded with this seal and testament—the Lord hath sworn and decreed that they shall be granted. Therefore, he giveth this promise unto you, with an immutable covenant that they shall be fulfilled; and all things wherewith you have been afflicted shall work together for your good, and to my name's glory, saith the Lord.
— D&C 98:1–3

There have been difficult times when we've all felt like saying, "I'm hanging on by a very thin thread!" And we may have even felt that thread we were dangling from was unraveling or about to snap. If we intertwine or braid the seven threads listed in the previous chapter to make them one, like a rope, no matter how thin it feels and no matter how desperate our situation, if we hold tight and don't let go, those threads will sustain us until help arrives and/or our situation changes. The holding tight may be the hardest part of the equation—to not give up.

Here is the concluding eighth powerful thread that guarantees success and safety: Patiently enduring.

That eighth thread may be compared to the knot in Franklin D. Roosevelt's statement, "When you come to the end of your rope, tie a knot and hang on!"

But let me explain what patiently enduring means and what it does not mean.

Patience is a noun. It is quiet, steady perseverance. Patience is synonymous with diligence. Patience, however, emphasizes calmness and the ability to tolerate delay. *Endure* is a verb. It means to carry on despite hardships. When we patiently endure, we have staying power. We obey God's commandments and faithfully wait for His will to be fulfilled. But this steadiness and waiting is not idle. The practice of patience does not mean we just turn it over to the Lord and sit and wait. It means we actively do our part through all the waiting. All those other threads—the seven previously listed—have to be active in our lives for patience to produce a positive outcome.

There is truth in Isaiah's promise, "They that wait upon the Lord shall renew their strength; they shall mount up with wings as eagles; they shall run, and not be weary; and they shall walk, and not faint" (Isaiah 40:31). When we're doing our part and patiently hang on, we are strengthened and our faith grows.

When we practice Christ-like patience, we trust the Lord will give us a positive outcome. It may not be immediate, but in time, we can watch it unfold. Sometimes "this" has to happen before "that" can come about. Heavenly Father sees the whole picture and answers all of our prayers. We only see the personal "me" picture—a tiny piece of the whole. But His choreography is universal and majestic, and His timing takes us all into account. God may not answer our prayers right away, but He is always on time—the right time!

Another thing about that positive outcome is that it isn't always what we expect or how we envision it. There again, His ways take all of us into account, and sometimes it takes a while for us to understand or to see the Lord's hand in our lives. Sometimes we have to remain trusting and patient because in this lifetime we may never come to understand why things worked out the way they did.

Patiently enduring does *not* mean we suffer unrestrained, blatant abuse. We must choose to see our surroundings for what they are—that's the awareness thread we talked about. With those things we are in control of, we are responsible to prayerfully allow awareness to drive our actions to safety.

These powerful threads presented in this book form a simple, proven pattern for success and safety, guaranteed. Making that statement does not diminish the intensity or severity of life's complications, but the pattern truly is simple. Consistently adhering to the pattern is what is hard.

To adhere means we stay attached; we are united by adhesion. On my daily walk, I pass a tree that was planted too close to the tall, wooden fence placed on the property line. Thus, in time, the trunk of the young tree grew over the fence, actually overlapping and adhering to the top edge. At this point, the tree and the fence cannot be separated. That is how we must be. We must adhere to our personal standards, calmly refusing to allow others to undermine our righteous efforts to become worthy heirs of our Father in Heaven. We must utilize the power that is within our grasp to determine what path our lives will take.

Adhering to those eight threads gives us Godly peace and security. And that kind of peace and security can see us through any challenge. We will be lifted to carry our burdens until help arrives. Our fears will be swallowed up, and we, in time, will recognize the hand of the Lord, paving the way for us to face our trials and find solutions.

These are the final days before the second coming of the Lord. It is crucial that we as Latter-day Saint women focus on the things that really matter. If we keep those eight threads as our focus, anything else of importance falls into its proper place.

In the Book of Mormon, Alma warned us to walk in humility, to strip ourselves of pride, envy, and backbiting (see Alma 5:27–35). He told us that we should repent of those things and accept God's invitation to live a righteous life. As we try to put our lives in order, we must be careful not to judge others. We are all imperfect. It is an on-going process, a goal, to be like Him. We all make mistakes, but Heavenly Father wants each of us to be happy and have joy. So he gave us a plan to make happiness possible, and He guides us step by step if we adhere to those threads of power and safety.

With each new day we have a clean slate to work on. We can attempt to right any wrongs we have committed, ask for forgiveness, and move ahead in a corrected pattern of living. Heavenly Father knows the pure intent of our hearts, recognizes our efforts day by day, and in His mercy measures them by the principle of seeing the half-full cup instead of the half-empty cup.

Elder Bruce R. McConkie stated in his book *Mormon Doctrine*:

> In carry forward his own purposes among men and nations, the Lord foreordained chosen spirit children in pre-existence and assigned them to come to earth at particular times and places so that they might aid in furthering the divine will. These pre-existence appointments, made 'according to the foreknowledge of God the Father' (1 Pet. 1:2), simply designated certain individuals to perform missions

which the Lord in his wisdom knew they had the talents and capacities to do . . . By their foreordination the Lord merely gives them the opportunity to serve him and his purposes if they will choose to measure up to the standard he knows they are capable of attaining.[1]

We are here now for a reason. The choreography of our Heavenly Father is unmistakable. We each have a job to do. We each have a valuable part in His plan. And we will be held accountable for the opportunities, gifts, and blessings we are given.

Joseph Smith said,

When the Master in the Savior's parable of the stewards called his servants before him he gave them several talents to improve on while he should tarry abroad for a little season, and when he returned he called for an accounting. So it is now. Our Master is absent only for a little season, and at the end of it He will call each to render an account; and where the five talents were bestowed, ten will be required; and he that has made no improvement will be cast out as an unprofitable servant, while the faithful will enjoy everlasting honors.[2]

It's easy to see that we cannot each be measured the same, because we are not the same. We will not be judged in comparison to each other. God knows what we are made of. He knows what He has given us. He knows what we are thinking and doing. We cannot rationalize nor excuse ourselves.

Through the ordinance of baptism, we covenant to take upon ourselves the name of Jesus Christ, to always remember Him, and to keep His commandments. As we keep our part of the covenant, the Spirit will always be with us. That is one of our Heavenly Father's most precious gifts to His daughters—the gift of the Holy Ghost. Through the power and companionship of the Holy Ghost, we can feel God's love and direction for us.

Satan wants us to think we are alone and that if we make a mistake, there's no way to correct it. But that's absolutely not true. Each week, when we take the sacrament, we commit to try harder, to do a better job of adhering those threads into our pattern of living. We have a fresh start every single day. We only fail if we don't try. And in the Lord's eyes, we always succeed when we do the best we can and try to improve each day. The Lord taught, "Ye are not able to abide the presence of God now, . . . wherefore, continue in patience until ye are perfected" (D&C 67:13).

Step by step, inch by inch, we move toward greater understanding and more exactness in keeping the commandments and our covenants. When we are hit by one of life's inevitable blows and feel like we're just "hanging on by a thread," let us make sure we're clinging to those seven braided threads with the knot at the end!

When we know the Lord is with us, we can handle with patience whatever comes. As we submit to and work with God's will for us, we can choose to be happy and feel the comfort and peace promised to the faithful.

As Paul the Apostle said, "Cast not away therefore your confidence, which hath great recompence of reward. For ye have need of patience, that, after ye have done the will of God, ye might receive the promise" (Hebrews 10: 35–36).

With so much drama happening around us in our world today, it's easy to dwell on the negative and lose sight of the positive. Healing powers of the body are released when we slow our pace enough to notice the uplifting beauty of God's creations. Even a short diversion, whether it's spontaneous or calculated, can ease tension and pressure, relax our body systems, and recharge and enlighten our minds. We can raise our level of happiness and calm by patiently putting our worries aside for a moment to notice the everyday, rejuvenating joys that surround us.

Early one summer morning as I walked down our narrow driveway, I happened to notice the lawn. It was covered with tiny droplets of dew. Each separate drop of moisture was a little, clear ball delicately balancing at the tip of a blade of green grass. I stooped down to marvel at the exquisite sight. Then I hurried back to the house. My youngest son was the only other person up and alert at home at that time. I asked him to come outside with me. He quickly put on his shoes and joined me in the front yard. Together we spontaneously smiled and enjoyed looking at and talking about one of the marvels of nature. Later, when I returned home from my errands, the dew had vanished. I realized I hadn't noticed those beautiful, individual balls like that before, yet they had been there at my feet often.

In the midst of turmoil and great heartache we have to purposely search out what is beautiful. When we slow our momentum and calm our fears sufficiently to see the beauty around us, we feel God's love and the sweet companionship of peace.

As the 13th Article of Faith states, "We believe all things, we hope all things, we have endured many things, and hope to be able to endure all things. If there is anything virtuous, lovely, or of good report or praiseworthy, we seek after these things."

Often the lovely and praiseworthy are found in nature, but if we look for them, they can also be found in the people around us—happy laughter between friends, a sincere compliment, the opportunity to serve others. I find the lovely and praiseworthy every time my granddaughter Ashlee comes to my house and gives me a hug. I look at her smiling face, and I see hope and love and trust. When we recognize and appreciate the beauty and goodness around us, even when our circumstances are difficult and uncertain, we can feel happiness in the present and hope for the future.

We are daughters of God. Our ultimate safety rests with the choices we make—the pattern we choose to follow in responding to the events in our lives. Anyone can smile and trust when life is easy. But our faith and character are tested when we face times of trial that require us to stretch and grow. It's not hard to pay tithing when we have plenty of money. The test is when we need the money. It's not hard to pray when we feel God has made life sweet for us. The test is when adversity hits and we still fall on our knees and thank Him for what we have. It's not hard to think we can accomplish all things when we're young and well. The test comes when our physical abilities are limited and we're called on to endure trials or loneliness we did not expect.

As our divine birthright, we must never forget our Eternal Father has a perfect love for us. He does keep His promises. He does hear our prayers. He does remember each of us. We are never alone. If we are faithful, He will see us through all our sad times of trial.

Since the restoration, faithful Latter-day Saint women, despite terrible things happening to them, have remained steady and true to the gospel. Their positive influences have been like blossoming branches reaching across the globe, helping other women wax strong in knowledge of the truth. Today, we have been committed to leave our footprints as evidence that we took the journey of life. No one else can do it like we can.

We are fully competent. We have reserves we cannot imagine and we must never underestimate our worth and our potential. Heavenly Father created us with all the skills and talents we need. We voted for agency. Now we just need to take the risk to make the choices that count. He will choreograph the happenings of our lives for our good. He created us to be queens. If we do all within our power, we can trust He will take care of the rest and provide a way for us to accomplish our work. As covenant-keeping women— daughters of God—He has complete confidence in us. And we can do it.

If we can place Christ at the center of our lives and trust He will guide and direct us, and not merely go through the motions but faithfully obey and serve him with all our hearts;

If we can pray and listen to the Holy Ghost, who prompts us with truth and reveals to us answers to our personal mysteries of stewardships;

If we can concentrate our energies with all the passion of our hearts to fulfill our righteous goals and desires, and along the way carry the shield of faith and acknowledge the arm and power of the Lord in all we do;

If we can resolve to achieve our divine mission even when the hard times come and obstacles seem to tower before us, and firmly renew our efforts with each new day;

If we can reverence motherhood, and magnify and honor our gifts from God;

If we can care for the body God gave us and nourish and develop our minds, and vow to be happy as we pursue our path to perfection;

If we can strive to be all that our experience prepares us to be, and not give up as we tire;

We can be calm and trust ourselves, even when others doubt us;

We can sense the Lord's guiding hand, and rejoice with Him in our victories;

We can report confidently to the God who knows all—who sees clearly where our hearts are—and we can experience the joy of associating with Gods, because the hope of eternal life is ours.

NOTES:

1. Elder Bruce R. McConkie, *Mormon Doctrine* (Salt Lake City: Bookcraft, 1966), 290.

2. Joseph Smith, *Teachings of the Prophet Joseph Smith*, compiled by Joseph Fielding Smith, Collector's Edition (American Fork: Covenant Communications, Inc.), 53.